50 hikes

in

Vermont

50 hikes in Vermont

Walks, Hikes, and Overnights
in the Green Mountain State

Fifth Edition

Bob Lindemann and Mary Deaett
for
THE GREEN MOUNTAIN CLUB

Backcountry Publications
Woodstock, Vermont

An Invitation to the Reader

Over time trails can be rerouted and signs and landmarks altered. If you find that changes have occurred on the routes described in this book, please let us know so that corrections may be made in future editions. The author and publisher also welcome other comments and suggestions. Address all correspondence to:

Editor, 50 Hikes™ Series
Backcountry Guides
PO Box 748
Woodstock, VT 05091

Library of Congress Cataloging-in-Publication Data
Lindemann, Bob.
    50 hikes in Vermont : walks, hikes, and overnights in the Green Mountain state / Bob Lindemann and Mary Deaett for the Green Mountain Club. — 5th ed.
       p.   cm. — (50 hikes series)
    Rev. ed. of: Fifty hikes in Vermont. 4th ed. c1990.
    Includes index.
    ISBN 0-88150-374-6
    1. Hiking—Vermont—Guidebooks. 2. Backpacking—Vermont—Guidebooks. 3. Vermont—Guidebooks. I. Deaett, Mary. II. Green Mountain Club. III. Title. IV. Series: Fifty hikes series.
GV199.42.V4L55   1997
917.43'0443—dc21   96-48311
                                                                            CIP

© 1990, 1997 by The Green Mountain Club
Fifth edition, third updated printing 1999

Published by Backcountry Guides,
a division of The Countryman Press
PO Box 748
Woodstock, VT 05091

Distributed by
W.W. Norton & Company Inc.
500 Fifth Avenue
New York, NY 10110

Page composition by Michael Gray
Series design by Glenn Suokko
Trail overlays by Richard Widhu
Cover photograph by Alden Pellett
Interior photographs by Bob Lindemann unless credited otherwise
Printed in the United States of America

Acknowledgments

As with any book, there are always a host of people who provide valuable assistance. Any Vermont hiking book would be difficult to write without the Green Mountain Club staff—we extend our sincere appreciation to them for helping us keep *50 Hikes in Vermont* as up-to-date as possible.

We would also like to thank the following: Ben Davis and Smith and Jan Edwards for reviewing the hikes; Mark Haughwout for checking southern hikes; Chris Wood for checking trailhead information; the United States Forest Service, including Fred Putnam and Sue Scott, Middlebury District; the Vermont Department of Forests, Parks and Recreation, especially Diana Frederick, Barre District, Laura Hollowell, and Rick White; Sharon O'Loughlin, geologist/information specialist, Agency of Natural Resources, for sending information on Mount Philo; John Wrazen, director of the Babcock Nature Preserve at Johnson State College; Don Whitney for sending information on the Ascutney Trails Association and Crystal Cascade; the Green Mountain Audubon Nature Center; and Reidun Nuquist for writing the history of the Green Mountains.

We would also like to acknowledge that much of the historical and geological information in this book was derived from State of Vermont, Agency of Natural Resources brochures and other publications. We are indebted to their research and cooperation in providing information to us.

Mary Deaett
Bob Lindemann
for the Green Mountain Club

50 Hikes at a Glance

		Location
Southern Vermont	1. Harmon Hill	east of Bennington
	2. Mount Olga	east of Wilmington
	3. Haystack Mountain	west of Wilmington
	4. Glastenbury Mountain	east of Bennington
	5. Stratton Pond	between Arlington and W. Wardsboro
	6. Stratton Mountain	between Arlington and W. Wardsboro
	7. Bald Mountain	north of Townshend Village
	8. Prospect Rock (Manchester)	east of Manchester
	9. Antone Mountain	west of Rupert
	10. Griffith Lake	south of Danby
	11. Green Mountain Trail	east of Danby
	12. White Rocks/Ice Beds	near Wallingford
	13. Clarendon Gorge	between Danby and Clarendon
	14. Mount Ascutney	west of Ascutney
Central Vermont	15. Okemo Mountain	west of Ludlow
	16. Pico Peak	at Sherburne Pass
	17. Deer Leap Mountain	at Sherburne Pass
	18. Appalachian Trail	near Woodstock
	19. Quechee Gorge	east of Woodstock
	20. Mount Independence	west of Orwell
	21. Mount Horrid Overlook	at Brandon Gap
	22. Rattlesnake Point	northeast of Brandon
	23. Robert Frost Trail	east of Ripton
	24. Texas Falls	west of Hancock
	25. Skylight Pond	east of Ripton
	26. Bread Loaf Mountain	south of Lincoln

Distance (in miles)	Vertical Rise (in feet)	Difficulty	View	Good for kids	Camping nearby	Good for winter	Notes
3.4	1265	M	✓			✓	snowshoeing
1.4	500	E/M	✓	✓	✓	✓	x-c skiing, snowshoeing, fire tower
4.8	1020	M	✓			✓	snowshoeing; parking difficult in winter
21.8	3640	S	✓		✓		overnight hike; need 2 cars; fire tower
7.8	660	M			✓	✓	x-c skiing, snowshoeing
9.0	1910	M/S	✓		✓	✓	strenuous snowshoeing, fire tower
3.5	1100	M/S	✓		✓	✓	showshoeing
3.0	1100	S	✓		✓	✓	
5.0	890	M		✓		✓	x-c skiing, snowshoeing, limited views
8.9	2340	S	✓		✓		
7.0	960	M/S	✓		✓	✓	x-c skiing
2.0	460	E	✓	✓		✓	snowshoeing
14.4	2775	E/M			✓		overnight hike; need 2 cars
6.0	2250	S	✓				
5.8	1900	M	✓			✓	snowshoeing, fire tower
5.4	1800	M	✓		✓		
2.0	700	E	✓	✓		✓	snowshoeing
21.6	5030	S	✓		✓		overnight hike; need 2 cars
1.5	250	E		✓	✓		
2.5	200	E/M		✓			interpretive center, historical interest
1.4	620	M	✓		✓	✓	snowshoeing, peregrine falcons
3.9	1160	M	✓		✓	✓	snowshoeing
1.0	120	E	✓	✓		✓	snowshoeing, x-c skiing
1.2	160	E		✓		✓	waterfalls
4.6	1620	M/S	✓		✓		
8.6	2235	S	✓		✓		

E=Easy; M=Moderate; S=Strenuous

50 Hikes at a Glance

	Location
Central Vermont *(cont.)* 27. Snake Mtn.	south of Addison
28. Mount Grant	south of Lincoln
29. Lincoln Gap	top of Lincoln Gap
30. Mount Abraham	east of Bristol
31. Monroe Skyline	between Lincoln and Appalachian Gaps
32. Spruce Mountain	south of Plainfield
33. Owl's Head	east of Marshfield
34. Mount Philo	north of Ferrisburg
35. Hires and Sensory Trails	near Huntington
36. Camel's Hump	west of Waterbury
37. Little River History Loop	west of Waterbury
38. Mount Hunger	east of Waterbury Center
39. Stowe Pinnacle	east of Stowe Village
40. Mount Worcester	north of Montpelier
41. Elmore Mountain	south of Morrisville
42. Mount Mansfield	north of Stowe
43. Sterling Pond	at Smuggler's Notch
44. Mount Pisgah	south end of Lake Willoughby
45. Mount Hor	south end of Lake Willoughby
46. Prospect Rock (Johnson)	west of Johnson
47. Ritterbush Camp	near Eden
48. Belvidere Mountain	north of Eden Mills
49. Jay Peak	east of Montgomery
50. Black Creek	north of Swanton

Northern Vermont (rows 32–50)

Distance (in miles)	Vertical Rise (in feet)	Difficulty	View	Good for kids	Camping nearby	Good for winter	Notes
3.5	980	M	✓			✓	
8.4	1960	S	✓	✓			
1.25	600	E/M	✓	✓			
5.2	2500	S	✓	✓			
11.1	2520	M	✓	✓			overnight hike; need 2 cars
4.5	1340	M	✓			✓	strenuous snowshoe
0.5	160	E	✓	✓	✓	✓	x-c skiing, showshoeing
0.5	50	E	✓	✓	✓	✓	x-c skiing, snowshoeing
1.25	200	E	✓	✓		✓	snowshoeing, museum and interpretive center
7.4	2645	S	✓		✓	✓	very strenuous showshoe
3.5	880	E/M			✓		historical interest, some x-c skiing
4.0	2330	M/S	✓			✓	strenuous snowshoe
2.8	1520	M	✓			✓	snowshoeing
5.0	1970	M	✓				solitude
4.5	1470	M	✓		✓	✓	snowshoeing
9.3	3825	M/S	✓		✓		overnight hike; highest peak in Vermont
6.5	1780	S	✓		✓		
2.5	1590	M	✓				peregrine falcons
3.5	1050	E/M	✓				
2.0	540	E	✓	✓		✓	snowshoeing
5.0	1040	M			✓	✓	
7.9	2100	S	✓		✓		fire tower
3.5	1680	M	✓		✓		
2.7	25	E		✓			

E=Easy; M=Moderate; S=Strenuous

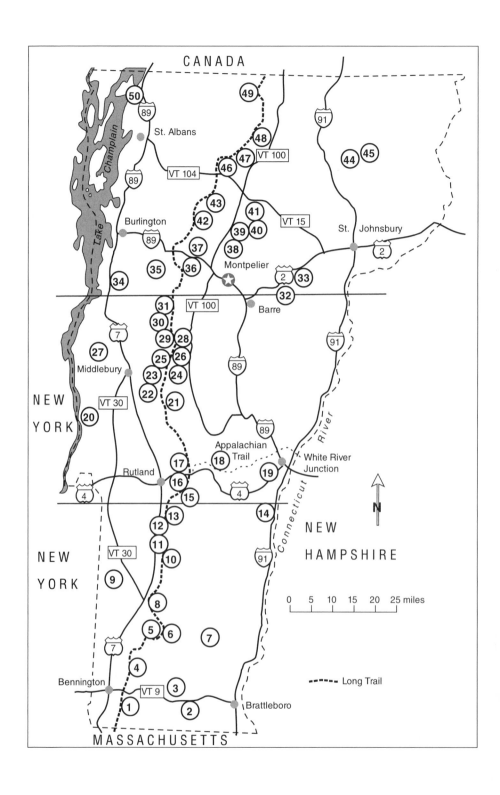

Contents

NORTHERN VERMONT

Foreword

For those who hike and enjoy the natural beauty of the Green Mountains, this new edition of *50 Hikes in Vermont* continues the Green Mountain Club tradition of providing up-to-date and reliable hiking information. Through the years, *50 Hikes in Vermont* has guided Vermonters and visitors alike to some of Vermont's most scenic and worthwhile hiking opportunities. Mary Deaett and Bob Lindemann continue to share their knowledge and expertise as Green Mountain Club volunteers who know and love the mountains of Vermont. We are grateful for their unselfish leadership and commitment. They represent the heart and soul of the Green Mountain Club—volunteers working hard to give others a chance to experience the beauty and splendor of Vermont's backcountry. On behalf of the Green Mountain Club and its nearly 6500 members, I would like to thank Mary, Bob, and Backcountry Publications for all the cooperation and support needed to produce this valuable guidebook.

Dennis L. Shaffer
Executive Director
The Green Mountain Club

Introduction

You are about to explore one of Vermont's greatest treasures—the Green Mountains. They offer hours and days of hiking enjoyment in late spring, summer, and fall.

This book guides you through the mountains along a variety of Vermont's hiking trails, from easy walks to ambitious day hikes to weekend backpacking trips. We have chosen both popular as well as some of the lesser known trails; some are quite simple, a few are very strenuous. All of these hikes offer you crisp mountain air and beautiful wilderness scenery, most with breathtaking views of surrounding pastoral valleys and neighboring mountain ranges. You can hike along sparkling streams, over suspension bridges, across open summits, and through ferned, secluded gulches. Choose the hikes that excite and appeal to you the most.

While we encourage your enthusiastic exploration of Vermont's hiking trails, we also caution you to consider your health and conditioning, your experience in the woods, the weather, your equipment, and a variety of other factors before exploring Vermont's backcountry wilderness. Please read the advice and information in the following section carefully before beginning your journey. Be prepared and be informed, and then thoroughly enjoy a safe journey into the Green Mountains of Vermont.

HOW TO USE THIS GUIDE

The hikes here are organized geographically to offer you a variety of hiking terrains and different scenery representing each region of the state. The general location, approximate distance and hiking time, vertical rise, difficulty rating, and the map that illustrates the area are listed at the beginning of each hike. This information is designed to help you select a hike that is within the limits of your hiking ability and the time available for your outing.

Total distance is the total number of miles you will hike on the trails described. Each hike description indicates clearly whether this distance refers to a loop, a return by the same route, or a one-way hike (with cars spotted at both ends of the trail).

Hiking time includes all time spent walking or climbing and some time for resting and enjoying the views. Allow extra time for meals and swimming or fishing in the streams and ponds en

The view toward Smugglers' Notch from the Mount Mansfield trail (Hike 42)

route. Times given are for a leisurely but steady pace and allow for differences in terrain. If you follow any alternate or side trails not included in the total distance, remember to adjust your hiking time accordingly.

Vertical rise is the total amount of climbing along the route. It may occur all in one climb, in which case it is the difference between the lowest and highest points on the route. But it may and frequently does occur over several climbs. If there are descents between these climbs, then the vertical rise noted for the hike will exceed the difference between the lowest and highest points on the hike. Substantial vertical rise can turn even a short hike into a real challenge.

Difficulty ratings are easy, moderate, and strenuous—with a few hikes falling in between. *Easy* hikes are accessible to most people, including first-time hikers, and are especially good for families with children. They are also appropriate when your hiking time may be limited but you still want to enjoy Vermont's beautiful scenery. *Moderate* hikes require a degree of stamina; some previous hiking experience is advisable. *Strenuous* hikes are challenging outings for experienced hikers in good physical condition.

Maps are listed at the beginning of each hike so that you can obtain supplements to the maps printed in this guide. The maps that appear in this book are based on United States Geological Survey (USGS) or Green Mountain National Forest (GMNF) topographic sheets.

Although the USGS maps are sometimes out of date, they may be helpful to you. They can be obtained from some sporting goods shops and bookstores, or you can order them by writing to: United States Geological Survey, Branch of Information Services, Box 25286, Denver Federal Center, Denver, CO 80225 (303-202-4700). You can also order USGS quads from two other sources. The National Survey, Topographic Office, Chester, VT 05143 (802-875-2121) stocks Vermont and New Hampshire quadrangles. Timely Discount Topos has access to USGS quads for all states. Timely Discount will take your order by phone (1-800-821-7609) and then ship your order the day after they receive your check or money order. All maps purchased through Timely Discount are on a prepaid basis only, but orders are fulfilled very quickly.

GMNF maps may be ordered from the Forest Supervisor's Headquarters, Green Mountain National Forest, 231 North Main Street, Rutland, VT 05701 (802-747-6700 or 747-6765 V/TDD). GMNF maps only include those quadrangles in which the forest is located. You must also send a prepaid order to receive these maps.

The maps in this book are intended only as general guides to the trails. Because of logging, development, and other wilderness disturbances, trail locations sometimes change, though every care is taken to ensure that trail descriptions and maps are accurate at the time of publication.

Before you begin your hike carefully plan your route, equipment, and supplies. Be sure to allow adequate time for unpredictable weather changes, and remember to leave a copy of your itinerary with a friend.

HIKING SEASON
The ideal time to hike in the Green Mountains is the summer and early fall. Most of the trails are not blazed for winter use and are, therefore, frequently impossible to follow.

Vermonters joke that spring never comes to Vermont—winter leads directly into "mud season"! When warmth does come to the valleys, trails in higher elevations become wet and muddy. Hiking during "mud season"—from mid-April to late May—can cause a great deal of damage to trails. Please wait until the trails are completely dry before hiking.

The average monthly temperature in June, July, and August is in the 60s, in September the high 50s, in October the 40s, and in early November the mid-30s. However, the temperature can drop below freezing at any time of the year!

Insects can be a problem throughout the late spring and summer. "Blackfly season" usually lasts from mid-May until mid-June, but blackflies can be a problem throughout the summer in certain locations. Mosquitoes are also a nuisance at dusk and dawn, especially in wet or swampy areas.

SAFETY

Vermont weather is extremely unpredictable, with the possibility of high-elevation snowstorms even in the summer! Rain and fog are common, and storms can be sudden and dangerous. If there is any threat of stormy weather, either do not hike at all or select a hike at a lower elevation, and be sure to bring adequate rain gear, a wool sweater, and a hat. Even on short hikes, always bring along a compass (learn how to use it first!), a first-aid kit, and a supply of prepared, high-energy foods like nuts and dried fruits.

Water can be polluted even in the most pristine mountain environments by an intestinal parasite called *Giardia lamblia.* Giardiasis is very unpleasant, often resulting in severe diarrhea and vomiting. Treat, boil, or filter all water before using or, for the majority of hikes in this book, simply carry water with you.

Unfortunately, vandalism of cars at trailheads is a problem; remove all valuables from your car, or at least lock them in your trunk.

Again, remember to leave your itinerary with a friend, stay on your planned route, and sign in at all registers. In case of a missing hiker, vandalism, or any other emergency, contact the Vermont State Police.

Most of the trails in this book are blazed with either white or blue paint. Important turns and intersections are indicated by arrows and double blazes (one blaze over the other). You should always be able to see the next blaze ahead of you. If you do not see a blaze after a few minutes, stop, look, and backtrack to make sure you are still on the trail.

CLOTHING AND EQUIPMENT

The most important rule for clothing, even in summer, is to dress in layers or bring extra clothing with you. The shirt that feels cool with perspiration on a hot summer day may chill you to the bone on the summit of a mountain where it is windy and cold. You should always take along an extra layer for protection.

Boots—Because most of the trails in this book are primitive footpaths, not specially surfaced trails, wear a good pair of boots that provide adequate support and traction.

Socks—Bring an extra pair in case your feet get wet.

Poncho or rainsuit—Remember, Vermont weather is unpredictable; always be prepared!

Sweater or jacket—For comfort and protection against winds and cooler temperatures at higher elevations.

Hat—40 percent of body heat is lost through your head.

Day pack

Guidebook, maps, and *compass*

Water bottle or *canteen*
First-aid kit (moleskin or similar product for blisters, Band-Aids in assorted sizes, triangular bandage or bandanna, adhesive tape, antiseptic cream, gauze)
Trail lunch (and extra food for emergencies)
Flashlight with working and extra batteries
Matches
Pocketknife
Insect repellent
Sunglasses (optional)
Camera and binoculars (optional)
Additional items required for backpacking trips:
Frame pack
Tent
Sleeping bag and pad
Stove and spare fuel
Cooking gear
Extra clothing
*Garbage bag*s (pack out *all* trash!)

TRAIL WORK
Many of the trails in Vermont's beautiful mountains have the added benefit of some man-made modifications—most of which make for drier hiking boots. The Civilian Conservation Corps (CCC), a government work program begun during the Great Depression of the 1930s, completed some of this work. Throughout this book you will see references made to the following terms:

Puncheon—Small wooden bridges on one or more log or board planks held off the ground on sills.

Turnpiking—A raised trail bed formed by placing logs on either side of the trail and filling between them with dirt and gravel.

Water Bars—A drainage system of log or rock construction and the best defense against trail erosion. Water bars are composed of three parts: the

bar, built of log or rock; the apron, a shallow slope to funnel water to the bar; and the ditch, which carries water from the bar and off the trail.

TRAIL COURTESY
Private Property—Many of the trails in this guide are located on private property. Please be considerate and appreciative of these landowners, and treat their property with respect to ensure that trails on private property remain open. Do not block traffic or access to private homes when parking at trailheads, and always be sure to check with landowners before parking on private property.

Dogs—Although your dog may be your best friend, please leave it at home. It is often difficult to prevent dogs from contaminating water supplies, and they frequently have problems with wildlife, especially porcupines. If you still choose to bring a dog with you, be sure to keep it leashed.

Trash and Waste—The Green Mountain Club has one firm trail motto: "Pack it in, pack it out." No litter should be left on the trail or in the woods. Because human waste can damage water quality, use outhouses when available, or otherwise bury human waste 6 inches deep at least 100 feet from any trail or water supply.

CAMPING AND FIRES
Camping and fires are restricted on most Vermont lands, depending on whether the land is private, state, or federal. Contact the Green Mountain National Forest, Vermont Department of Forests, Parks and Recreation, or the Green Mountain Club for more information.

PEREGRINE FALCONS
The following trails in this book pass by the nesting sites of peregrine fal-

cons: White Rocks (Hike 12), Mount Horrid Overlook (Hike 21), Elephants Head (Hike 43), and Mount Pisgah (Hike 44). Falcons are very sensitive to human disturbance, especially from above, and may abandon their nests if they are at all approached. Therefore, some of the trails are closed during their nesting season, which runs from February through mid-July. They should be watched only from a great distance, using either powerful binoculars or a telescope.

Peregrine falcons have finally returned to Vermont after a 30-year absence. These beautiful birds were almost eliminated by the use of the pesticide DDT after World War II. After DDT was banned in 1972, the Peregrine Fund at Cornell University and the United States Fish and Wildlife Service started a reintroduction program. Captive-born young falcons were released on many cliff sites throughout the East. The peregrine release, or "hacking," program in Vermont is sponsored by the Vermont Institute of Natural Science, the Vermont Department of Fish and Wildlife, and the United States Forest Service. The first wild nesting pair returned to Vermont at Mount Pisgah in 1985.

Bringing these magnificent birds back to Vermont is extremely important. Please obey any posted signs, and do not disturb the birds.

ARCTIC-ALPINE VEGETATION
Several of the higher summits in this guidebook are home to unique ecosystems with fragile arctic-alpine plant communities. This rare and beautiful plant life remains from an era when ice sheets covered northern New England.

When the most recent glaciers retreated between 8000 and 12,000 years ago, arctic plants grew in exposed areas. As the climate warmed, most of the plants died—except for those on a few mountaintops where the climate resembles the Arctic regions 1000 miles to the north of Vermont. Shallow soils, high winds, low temperatures, a short growing season, high precipitation (100 or more inches a year), and heavy fog (the alpine plants absorb 5 to 30 inches of fog moisture each year in addition to precipitation) allow only a few species to survive. Those that remain grow very slowly. For example, it takes approximately 80 years for a tree near the timberline to grow 2 inches in diameter.

The survival of this rare vegetation, much of which looks like ordinary grass, is precarious. The same shallow soil and vigorous climatic conditions that allow it to grow make the environment especially vulnerable to hiker disturbances. When a small portion of alpine tundra is destroyed, the wind rapidly scours large holes in the damaged turf, and the soil quickly erodes. Removal of rocks from the grassy tundra is especially harmful in this respect. Fires destroy not only the ground cover plants, but also the thin underlying layer of humus. Because excessive trampling of plants and soil leads to further loss of rare vegetation, be especially vigilant to stay on the marked trails and rock outcrops.

THE GREEN MOUNTAINS
The Green Mountains were part of an extensive inland sea until approximately 350 million years ago, when pressure and heat transformed this region into a high-mountain range. The mountains were then shaped and formed, until just 12,000 years ago, by 1000-foot-thick Ice Age glaciers.

The average elevation of today's Green Mountain ridgeline is 2000 feet,

Along the Appalachian Trail (Hike 18)

although five peaks exceed 4000 feet: Mount Mansfield (4393), Killington Peak (4241), Mount Ellen (4083), Camel's Hump (4083), and Mount Abraham (4006).

Below 2400 feet, you will find a mixture of northern hardwoods like sugar maple and beech. A transitional forest, which occurs between 2400 and 3000 feet, includes yellow and white birch and red spruce. Above 3000 feet balsam fir dominates along with some remaining red spruce.

The Green Mountains have long played an important part in the lives of Vermonters. In addition to being an abundant source of clean, fresh water, they are vital as a timber and recreational resource. While significant numbers of Europeans didn't settle in Vermont until the end of the French and Indian War (1763), archaeological finds document the presence of Native Americans as far back as the Paleoindian period, or about 8500 BC Abenakis lived and foraged here, as well as Iroquois. The richest sites have been excavated in the Champlain Valley in northwest Vermont, along the rivers draining into Lake Champlain, and in the Connecticut River valley. State archaeologists constantly add to our knowledge of Native American history.

European settlers were of predominantly Anglo-Saxon stock and came north from Connecticut and Massachusetts for the cheap and plentiful land. They settled where the land was most fertile; like the Abenakis, they chose the Champlain lowlands and the Connecticut River valley. They also cleared land along Vermont's first two roads, Crown Point Military Road and Bayley-Hazen Military Road, both of which traversed the Green Mountains. In 1791, the first Vermont census reported 85,000 people living here.

The population boom, however, was short-lived. The rocky state was largely unsuited for farming, and when the Erie Canal opened in 1825, westward migration began. People became a major export along with potash, wool, lumber, dairy products, granite, and marble. Today the cellar holes and stone walls encountered by hikers on the lower slopes of the Green Mountains are all that remain of abandoned farms.

The mountains, once an obstacle to east–west travel, have become an economic asset. Within easy driving distance of major population centers on the eastern seaboard, they are visited by thousands of skiers, hikers, hunters, snowmobilers, and bicyclists every year; tourism is now a major industry in Vermont.

THE GREEN MOUNTAIN CLUB
Since its founding in 1910, the Green Mountain Club's primary purpose has been to build, maintain, and protect hiking trails and shelters for the enjoyment of Vermont's residents and visitors.

In 1910 the GMC founded the Long Trail (LT), the nation's oldest long-distance hiking trail. In addition to the 270-mile LT, which follows the ridgeline of the Green Mountains from Massachusetts to Canada, the Long Trail System also encompasses over 175 miles of side trails and 62 rustic cabins and lean-tos. This entire system is managed and maintained by Green Mountain Club seasonal field personnel, permanent staff, and hundreds of dedicated volunteers, in cooperation with private landowners and state and federal agencies.

In 1985, the GMC learned that 34 of the 65 miles of the Long Trail on private land in northern Vermont were for sale. Rising real estate values, the unsettled economics of the forest products industry, and rapid development in Vermont have created a volatile land market. The GMC also faced serious problems with landowners who wanted the Long Trail removed from their property or who wanted to use the land for purposes incompatible with the trail.

The Green Mountain Club was convinced that the scenic quality, environment, wildlife habitat, and continuity of the Long Trail had to be saved. Consequently, the Long Trail Protection Campaign was started and important results have been achieved. As of August 1998, over $6 million has been raised, and 48.5 miles of the Long Trail in northern Vermont, 14 miles of side trails, and 17,856 acres of backcountry land have been permanently protected.

The effort to save the Long Trail must continue. Vermont is experiencing a construction and population boom as well as tremendous pressures on land use. Eleven miles of the Long Trail and 6 miles of side trails are still in need of protection. The Green Mountain Club will continue the effort to preserve these high mountain lands that are so important to Vermonters and the thousands of people who visit the state each year.

Membership in the Green Mountain Club is the best way for you to support the protection and preservation of the Long Trail System, and the GMC is open to anyone interested in hiking and in Vermont's mountains.

If you would like to be involved in local outdoor and trail activities, you may join one the GMC's sections (chapters). Each section schedules hikes, other outings and social events, and is responsible for maintaining a specific portion of the Long Trail. You may also choose to become an at-large member if you are interested in supporting the Green Mountain Club,

but not interested in joining a section. Benefits are the same for both types of membership: a subscription to the GMC's quarterly newsletter, *The Long Trail News;* discounts on hiking maps, guidebooks, and other publications; and reduced fees at many GMC overnight camping sites or shelters.

If you would like more information on the Green Mountain Club, the trails in this book, or other hiking opportunities in Vermont, please contact us. We will be happy to help you plan your next hiking adventure.

The Green Mountain Club
Route 100, RR 1, Box 650
Waterbury Center, VT 05677
(802) 244-7037

HIKING INFORMATION AVAILABLE FROM THE GREEN MOUNTAIN CLUB
The Green Mountain Club issues a variety of publications about hiking and backpacking in Vermont and welcomes inquiries about trail conditions and planning. To order the GMC publications listed below, see the order form in the back of this book.

Guidebooks and Maps
Long Trail Guide (24th Edition 1996)— All-new edition with 16 color topographical maps. Complete description of the Long Trail, its side trails and shelters, and the Appalachian Trail in Vermont; suggested hikes, helpful hints, and winter use suggestions.

Day Hiker's Guide to Vermont (3rd Edition 1987, Sixth Printing 1995)— Companion volume to the *Long Trail Guide.* Comprehensive coverage of more than 200 short hikes throughout the state; 12 color topographical maps and 34 black-and-white maps; hiking tips and suggestions.

Mt. Mansfield (1995)—Color, foldout topographical map of the Mount

Mansfield area; weather resistant, with trail mileages, overnight facilities, trailheads, regulations, and other information.

Mount Mansfield Booklet
Tundra Trail—A Self-Guiding Walk: Life, Man and the Ecosystem on Top of Mt. Mansfield, Vermont—This 12-page booklet with illustrations describes a natural history hike along the Long Trail on the summit ridgeline of Mount Mansfield.

Green Mountain Club History
Green Mountain Adventure, Vermont's Long Trail (1st Edition 1985, Second Printing 1989)—An illustrated history of the Green Mountain Club by Jane & Will Curtis and Frank Lieberman. Ninety-six pages of rare black-and-white photographs and anecdotes of the GMC's first 75 years.

Pamphlets
The Long Trail: A Footpath in the Wilderness—Brochure with information and suggestions on hiking the Long Trail. Free with legal-sized SASE.
   Winter Trail Use in the Green Mountains—Brochure containing basic information about using the Long Trail System in winter. Free with legal-sized SASE.

OTHER RESOURCES
For additional information on hiking in Vermont, you may wish to contact one or more of the following organizations.

On Federal Lands
Green Mountain National Forest
   Forest Supervisor's Office
231 North Main Street, Route 7
Rutland, VT 05701
802-747-6700

On State Lands
Department of Forest, Parks, and
   Recreation
Agency of Natural Resources
103 South Main Street
Waterbury, VT 05671-0601
802-241-3655

On the Appalachian Trail *(AT Guide to New Hampshire and Vermont)*
Appalachian Trail Conference
799 Washington Street
PO Box 807
Harpers Ferry, WV 25425
304-536-6331

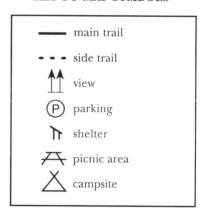

KEY TO MAP SYMBOLS

——	main trail
- - -	side trail
⋀⋀	view
Ⓟ	parking
⋔	shelter
⊼	picnic area
⋀	campsite

SOUTHERN VERMONT

1

Harmon Hill

Total distance: 3.4 miles

Hiking time: 3 hours

Vertical rise: 1265 feet

Rating: Moderate

Maps: GMNF Woodford, Bennington, Pownal, Stamford

This hike features an elaborate set of stone steps that ascend from the VT 9 valley plus extensive views of Bennington and the Taconic Mountain Range. You also see the monument that commemorates the August 16, 1777 Battle of Bennington.

How to Get There
The trailhead is located at the Long Trail/Appalachian Trail (LT/AT) parking lot on the north side of VT 9, 4.5 miles east of Bennington. Parking for 25 or more cars is available in this lot on the north side of the highway. A "Green Mountain National Forest" sign marks the trailhead on the south side of VT 9.

The Trail
Begin your hike heading south on the white-blazed LT/AT. The trail enters the woods at a double blaze, turns right, and begins a long, steep ascent up stone steps. Climb quickly to a moss-covered boulder and outcrop; then traverse the first level section before climbing more stone steps. The road can be seen below you as you gain elevation. At 0.2 mile you begin a series of long switchbacks, moving from one set of steps to another as you ascend out of the valley.

Light through the trees indicates that the climb is almost finished as you near the top of the ridge. At 0.6 mile the trail levels and descends slightly through a forest of primarily maple, birch, and oak trees. This area provides a welcome contrast to the climb you just completed. You soon cross a tiny brook and enter a fern meadow. As you return to the forest, you reach a long set of puncheon at 1.0 mile. Cross another wet area on puncheon and stones, and ascend through a darker, denser woods.

At 1.5 miles you come to another fern meadow with sunlight filtering through the trees. Soon the meadow opens up even more, and Bald Mountain ridge can be seen to the northwest. Raspberries growing along the

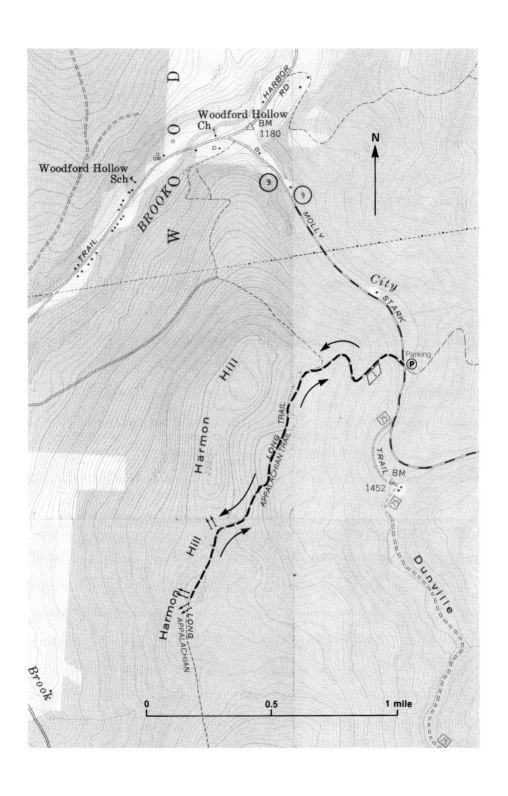

The Long Trail going over Harmon Hill

trail should be ripe in late July. You pass through tall ferns before you reach the 2325-foot summit at 1.7 miles. Spur trails lead to views of Bennington, the Monument, the Taconic Range, and Mount Anthony. The large meadow is kept open through the use of con-trolled burns by the United States Forest Service.

To return, follow the same trail back down to your car. Be careful through the wet areas and on the steps, which are almost as difficult to descend as they are to ascend.

2

Mount Olga

Total distance; 1.4-mile loop

Hiking time 1½ hours

Vertical rise: 500 feet

Rating: Easy to moderate

Map: USGS 7.5' Wilmington

The trail up Mount Olga is located in Molly Stark State Park, which was named after the wife of General John Stark. During the Revolutionary War in 1777, the general sent Molly a message asking her to "send every man from the farm that will come and let the haying go." Molly organized their farm men and, along with 200 other men, went to the general's aid. After the Battle of Bennington, General Stark returned home with one of the six brass cannons captured from the British as a token of gratitude to Molly.

This park, one of the smaller ones in the state park system, is a beautiful place to picnic or camp. A day-use fee is charged.

How to Get There
Molly Stark State Park is 3.4 miles east

of Wilmington on VT 9. Ample parking is available.

The Trail
You may want to pick up the free park brochure *Hiking Trail to Mount Olga* before beginning your hike. The trail begins on the east side of the park road opposite the caretaker's home, next to the park entrance building. A sign indicates a distance of 0.7 mile to the fire tower. Follow the blue-blazed trail down a short embankment on steps, across a small wooden bridge over a stream, and up through a stately spruce forest. The wide trail is covered with a soft carpet of needles. You soon cross over an old stone wall and continue your ascent until you reach a left arrow. Turn left, pass among boulders and ferns, and then cross the remains of another low stone wall.

Climb again on moderate grades until you reach a boulder and a rough-barked maple tree growing on the left side of the trail. This tree has four distinct large trunks and several smaller trees growing out of its crotch. The trail narrows, becomes steeper, and, at 0.6 mile, reaches a junction on your right. From the junction, the trail bears left and steeply ascends to the 2415-

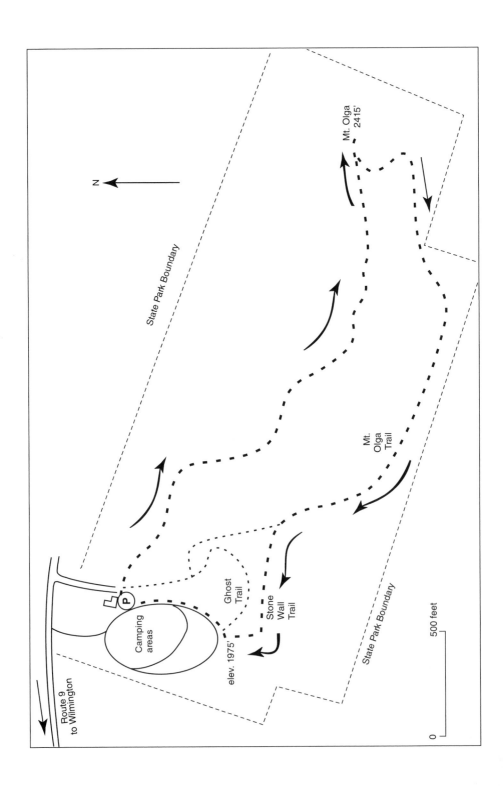

N ←

State Park Boundary

Mt. Olga 2415'

Mt. Olga Trail

State Park Boundary

Ghost Trail

Stone Wall Trail

elev. 1975'

Camping areas

P

Route 9 to Wilmington

500 feet

0

foot wooded summit, which has a fire tower, three old buildings, and a radio relay tower.

The summit was established as a fire lookout, with a wooden tower, in the early 1930s. In 1949–50 the wooden tower was removed, and the steel tower from Bald Mountain in Townshend was transferred to Mount Olga. This tower, which is still standing, was abandoned as a fire lookout in the 1970s. Climb the fire tower for a beautiful 360-degree panoramic view of southern Vermont, including Haystack Mountain, Mount Snow, and the Harriman Reservoir. You can also see into northwestern Massachusetts.

Return to the trail junction, turn left on the return loop, and descend on easy grades through numerous rock outcrops. Swinging right, you approach the park boundary, marked by red tape on the trees. At the junction you follow the Stone Wall Trail, continuing through a mixed forest on easy grades, between giant boulders and ledges, and across a wet area on planks. You pass the Ghost Trail junction at 1.3 miles. Continue downhill on the Stone Wall Trail, parallel to an old stone wall, through overgrown pastureland that is sometimes quite wet. The old stone wall and trail soon turn right and reach the campground road near campsite #10. Turn right and follow the road back to your car at 1.4 miles.

3

Haystack Mountain

Total distance: 4.8 miles

Hiking time: 3 hours

Vertical rise: 1020 feet

Rating: Moderate

Map: USGS 7.5' Mount Snow

Rock outcroppings on the summit of Haystack Mountain provide beautiful views of southern Vermont and south-western New Hampshire.

How to Get There

Care is needed to find the trailhead, which is located in the Chimney Hills development northwest of Wilmington. From the traffic light in Wilmington (0.0), drive 1.1 miles west on VT 9. Turn right (north) on Haystack Road, and at 1.4 miles bear right, continuing to follow paved Haystack Road. At 2.35 miles you reach an intersection where you turn left and follow the sign for Clubhouse and Chimney Hill Roads. At the next intersection, at 2.5 miles, turn right on dirt Binney Brook Road. Bear left at the next three intersections. At 3.5

miles, turn right on Upper Dam Road. Continue for a short distance on this road to a left turn at 3.6 miles. At 3.8 miles you reach the trailhead, marked on your right with an orange arrow pointing up the trail. Parking for about five cars is available along the road. Please do not block driveways or park on private property.

The Trail

Your pathway, which follows an old road on easy to moderate grades, is sporadically marked with blue plastic diamonds. At the beginning of the trail, a yellow gate blocks vehicles from driving up the road. Watch on your left for Binney Brook, which is the outlet for Haystack and Crystal Ponds, and a galvanized spring pipe visible across the brook. At 0.75 mile the trail leaves the old road, which continues about 1.5 miles to Crystal and Haystack Ponds. The trail turns left and follows the Deerfield Ridge Trail, used extensively in the winter by snow-mobilers and cross-country skiers. This section is marked for snowmobile use with orange blazes.

At 1.1 miles the trail turns right at a prominent orange arrow. Look for chipmunks and squirrels in the beech

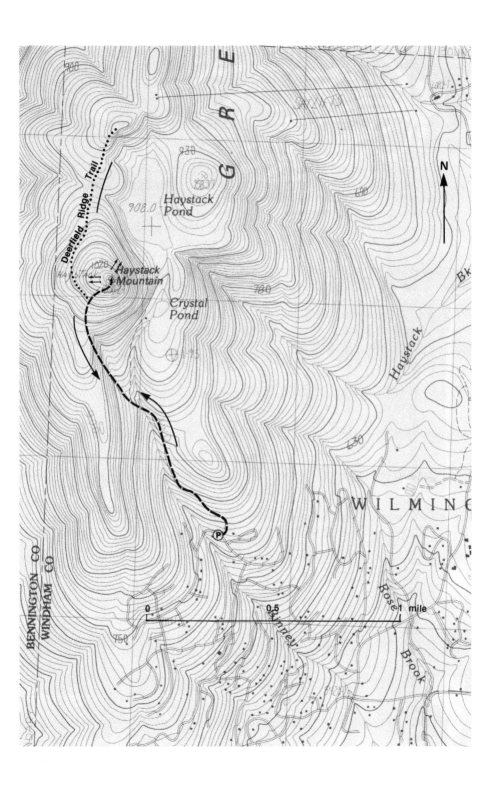

stand. The trail now climbs more gradually along the ridge. At 1.6 miles you reach a small promontory with Haystack Mountain visible straight ahead. You soon pass through a hemlock stand with views through the trees to the west.

Bear right and continue to climb north along the ridge with unobstructed views to the west. Enter a boggy section, before gradually climbing through an evergreen stand. Enjoy the fresh balsam scent!

As the trail descends and skirts the southwestern edge of the mountain, you pass between two rock outcrops. Just beyond the rocks, you reach the intersection of the trail to Haystack Mountain. Turn right on this trail and ascend along the densely forested summit ridge until you reach a trail junction at 2.2 miles. Bear left and continue along the blue-blazed trail, which ascends to another junction. Bear left again to the wooded summit at 2.4 miles. (Remember to note where the trail enters the summit.)

Two rock outcrops provide views to the north of Haystack Pond, the Haystack Mountain Ski Area, and the summit of Mount Snow. To the south you can see the Harriman Reservoir; to the southwest, Mount Greylock, the highest mountain in Massachusetts; to the west, the fire tower on the summit of Glastenbury Mountain; and, to the east, Monadnock Mountain in New Hampshire.

After enjoying the view, hike back down the same trail to your car.

4

Glastenbury Mountain and West Ridge Loop

Total distance: 21.8-mile loop

Hiking time: 2 days, 1 night

Vertical rise: 3640 feet

Rating: Strenuous

Maps: GMNF Woodford, Bennington

There are few opportunities on Vermont's Long Trail for loop backpacking trips. This hike, through remote forests and over several mountains, is an excellent exception.

Your first day, follow the Long Trail and Appalachian Trail (LT/AT) north from VT 9 through a very isolated forest to Goddard Shelter and the summit of Glastenbury Mountain. A summit fire tower provides spectacular views of southern Vermont. The second day, you hike south on the West Ridge Trail to the summit of Bald Mountain and then back to VT 9.

How to Get There

The trailhead, marked with a sign, is on the north side of VT 9, 5.2 miles east of Bennington and approximately 1 mile west of Woodford.

The Trail

Day One

Total distance 10.1 miles

Hiking time: 6 hours

Vertical rise: 2640 feet

From the parking area, take the white-blazed LT/AT north, parallel to and then across City Stream on the William A. McArthur Bridge. The bridge was built in 1977 by the United States Forest Service (USFS) in memory of a Green Mountain Club member who helped to maintain the trails in this area. Follow the stream a short distance, bear right, and begin a very steep ascent up the ridgeline. You can still see evidence of the small tornado that devastated this hillside in 1988. Utilizing a series of rocky switchbacks, you climb rapidly out of the VT 9 valley.

At 0.6 mile you pass through a split rock before you begin a moderate ascent. Cross two old roads, first a small one and then a larger one, at 1.1 miles.

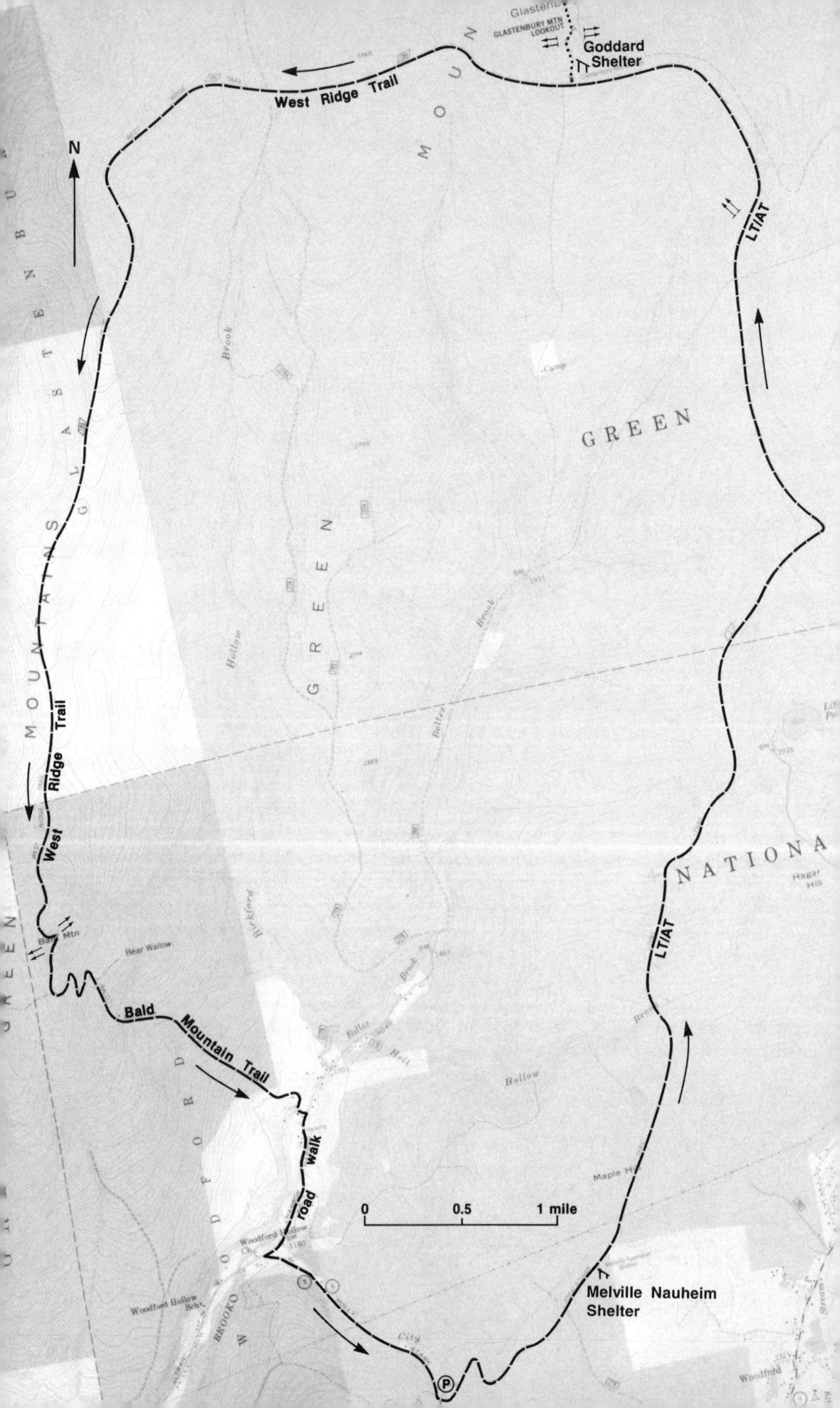

Glastenbury

GLASTENBURY MTN
LOOKOUT

Goddard
Shelter

West Ridge Trail

N

LT/AT

G R E E N

M O U N T A I N

G L A S T E N B U R Y   M O U N T A I N S

West Ridge Trail

Bear Wallow

Bald Mountain Trail

road walk

Woodford Hollow
Ch.

Woodford Hollow Sch.

B R O O K O

W O O D F O R D

City

P

N A T I O N A

Hagar
Hill

Maple H

LT/AT

Melville Nauheim
Shelter

0   0.5   1 mile

Woodford

You soon reach a spur trail on the right at 1.7 miles, which leads 200 feet to the Melville Nauheim Shelter. The shelter, constructed in 1977 by the Bennington Section of the Green Mountain Club, is a good place to rest.

Return to the trail junction and continue north over slightly easier grades to a power-line cut on Maple Hill at 2.0 miles. Take time to enjoy the views of Bennington and Mount Anthony to the west, Mount Snow and Haystack Mountain to the east. Continue uphill to the top of Maple Hill and then descend across a wet area on puncheon. Now on rolling terrain, the trail leads you across Hell Hollow Brook on a bridge at 3.1 miles. Camping is not permitted in this area because the brook is part of the Bennington public water supply.

Beyond the brook, continue your ascent across a swamp filled with balsam and spruce trees and up the ridge to a lookout at 4.3 miles. The lookout is a nice place to stop for lunch while gazing across the valley to Haystack Mountain.

After lunch, continue on rolling terrain over two hills to the 3100-foot summit of Little Pond Mountain at 5.5 miles and Little Pond Lookout. With Glastenbury Mountain still in the distance, you climb over two minor summits and along the ridgeline to Glastenbury Lookout at 7.4 miles. From this overlook you see the summit of Glastenbury ahead, your destination for the first day. Descend into and then out of an overgrown sag. The trail soon gets very steep as you climb the mountain on steps. Cross a spring and reach Goddard Shelter at 9.8 miles.

Goddard Shelter, the third shelter at the same site on Glastenbury, was built in 1985. The first shelter was built of tin in 1929 and the second of logs in 1965. In 1983, Ted Goddard Jr. made a generous financial offer to help build a new shelter in memory of his father. Almost all of the materials were cut on site, but because the native balsam fir trees were not in the best health, dimension lumber for flooring and roofing materials had to be airlifted to the site by the Vermont Air National Guard.

After you settle in and eat dinner, take a short, 0.3-mile trip to the wooded summit of Glastenbury Mountain. The fire tower, built in 1927 by the Vermont Timberland Owners' Association, was abandoned in the late 1940s and later renovated by the USFS as an observation deck for hikers. From the tower you have a breathtaking 360-degree view of the surrounding wilderness. You can see Mount Equinox and Stratton Mountain to the north; Haystack Mountain, Mount Snow, and the Somerset Reservoir to the east. Return to the shelter for a much-needed and welcome good night's rest.

Day Two

Total distance: 11.7 miles

Hiking time: 7 hours

Vertical rise: 1000 feet

If you are an early riser, climb the summit tower to enjoy a spectacular sunrise and a blanket of mist in the valley below. Eat breakfast, load your pack, and look for the blue-blazed West Ridge Trail just west of the shelter. Take this initially obscure trail down the western ridge of the mountain. Bear left and continue your descent with limited views back to Glastenbury Mountain and of the valley below. There are very few blazes along this hillside, so be sure to stay on the trail.

Trail up Glastenbury Mountain

Ascend over a crest, and then begin a long descent to an old logging road where you turn right, walk a few yards, and turn left back into the woods. Hike around a beaver pond and up to a major logging road at 2.5 miles. Turn right on the road, walk a few yards, turn left up the steep bank, and begin a very long, steep climb to a 3423-foot minor summit. As you hike along the ridge, the blazes are easier to follow. Pass through a stand of dense hemlocks before returning to mixed hardwoods and a more open forest. The trail is quite rocky as you hike along the hillside.

The summit of Bald Mountain is reached at 7.7 miles. Although wooded, the summit is long and flat, with numerous views and light-colored rocks. Try to spot the route you just hiked between Glastenbury Mountain (with the fire tower) and this peak. Enjoy views of Mount Greylock to the south and of the Taconic Range to the west.

The West Ridge Trail ends at a junction with the Bald Mountain Trail. A right turn leads east to Bennington. You turn left on the Bald Mountain Trail and begin a steep, rocky descent to a USFS trail sign and spur trail to Bear Wallow (a spring). The trail now follows an old road intersected by numerous old logging roads. At the red-blazed USFS boundary, turn right and descend along the roadway. You pass a registration box and start to see signs of civilization. At 9.7 miles you reach the Bald Mountain trailhead parking area and a public road. Turn right and follow the road to VT 9 in Woodford Hollow at 10.5 miles. Turn left on VT 9, and hike back to your car in the LT/AT parking area at 11.7 miles.

5

Stratton Pond

Total distance: 7.8 miles

Hiking time: 5 hours

Vertical rise: 660 feet

Rating: Moderate

Map: GMNF Londonderry SW

This long but almost level hike leads to Stratton Pond, which is located in the 15,680-acre Lye Brook Wilderness. There are few trails through this heavily forested wilderness, but several lakes, streams, and bogs dot the landscape. The wilderness contains beautiful waterfalls and meadows, as well as the remnants of old logging railroads and sawmills. "The Burning," the site of a large fire around the turn of the century, is located in the western portion of the wilderness. It is a popular spot for wildlife such as wild turkey, white-tailed deer, and black bear.

How to Get There

The trail is located on the north side of the Arlington–West Wardsboro Road (also known as the Kelley Stand Road). From VT 100 in West Wards-boro (0.0), drive 8.2 miles west on the Arlington–West Wardsboro Road to the intersection of United States Forest Service (USFS) Road–FR 71. A parking lot on FR 71 just east of the intersection has space for 10 to 15 cars. A wooden USFS sign and information board mark the trailhead.

The Trail

This blue-blazed trail follows the former route of the Long Trail/Appalachian Trail (LT/AT). Note the extensive trail work, including water bars, puncheon, and turnpiking.

Begin your hike across puncheon and over turnpiking through a young beech and softwood forest. The trail, now resembling a boardwalk through the woods, ascends slightly and crosses several wet areas on puncheon. At 1.0 mile cross an old red-blazed property line, descend slightly through white birches, and come to an open area with ferns. Descend again at 1.5 miles on puncheon across another wet area, and enter a birch forest. This area is quite beautiful on a sunny day, with sunlight filtering through the trees.

At 2.3 miles you cross an old road, enter a dark, dense softwood forest,

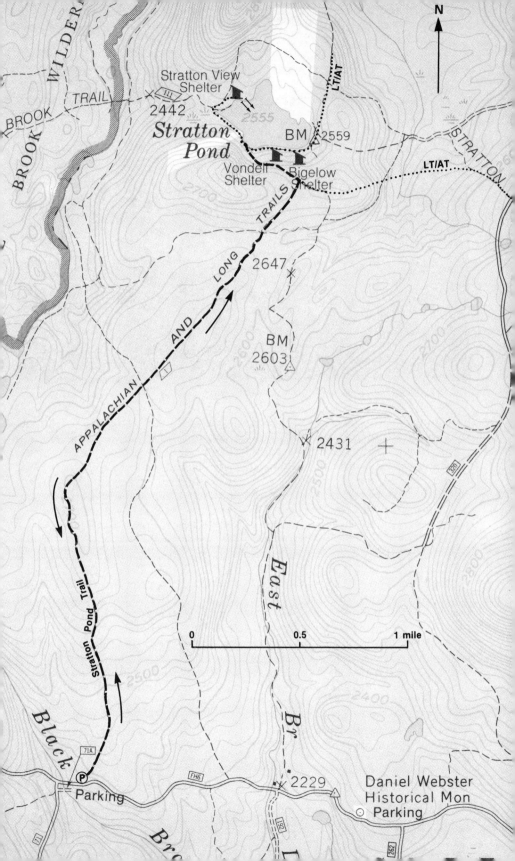

The view to Stratton Mountain from Bromley Mountain

and climb five wooden steps to return to a sunnier, more open hardwood forest. As you begin a gradual ascent, notice the large stumps that indicate the size of the trees once logged in this area. Cross another wet area on puncheon, and look on your right for a large birch with roots engulfing a boulder. Continue your hike through a small softwood forest, across more puncheon, and past a large moss-covered boulder.

At 3.8 miles you cross a small brook on stepping-stones. Look for a double blaze, where you turn left and descend a rocky, wet old logging road to the junction of the LT/AT. A USFS sign indicates that Stratton Mountain is 2.6 miles from this junction.

Follow the LT/AT north to the shore of Stratton Pond. Stratton Pond, the largest body of water on the Long Trail, is one of the highest overnight-use areas on the trail. There are over 2000 overnight hikers at the pond between Memorial Day and Columbus Day. The use is concentrated along the pond's shoreline, which is particularly prone to damage. The pond, where you can swim and fish, is 30 feet deep at the deepest point, and an average of 10 feet deep overall. Most of the pond and surrounding lands were acquired by the USFS in 1985. A Green Mountain Club caretaker is stationed at the site during the hiking season to assist hikers and maintain the trails and shelters. Please follow the caretaker's instructions to help protect this valuable natural area.

An information board at the pond describes a 1.4-mile loop trail around the pond, which you may wish to explore if you have time. After exploring the pond area, return via the same trails on which you set out.

6

Stratton Mountain

Total distance: 9-mile loop

Hiking time: 7 hours

Vertical rise: 1910 feet

Rating: Moderately strenuous

Map: GMNF Londonderry SW

This long, beautiful hike has several scenic overlooks of Somerset Reservoir and Stratton Pond as well as nice views from the summit tower. You can also hike out and back the same trail in 6.8 miles for a shorter trip.

Stratton Mountain played an important role in the conception of both the Long Trail and the Appalachian Trail. On Stratton Mountain in 1909, James P. Taylor thought about a "long trail" that would link the summits of the Green Mountains. Several years later on the same mountain, Benton MacKaye was inspired to develop an entire trail system along the Appalachian Mountains from Georgia to Maine.

How to Get There

Take VT 100 to the junction of Arlington–West Wardsboro Road (or Kelley Stand Road) in West Wardsboro (0.0). Drive 7.1 miles west on Arlington–West Wardsboro Road to the Long Trail/Appalachian (LT/AT) parking lot on the north side of the road. There is parking space for 8 to 10 cars. A "United States Forest Service (USFS)" sign marks the trailhead.

The Trail

Begin your hike north along the white-blazed LT/AT up the bank behind the parking area. You quickly enter the woods and climb onto a small knob. Numerous old logging roads intersect the trail, and, at times, you follow them for a short distance, crossing several wet areas on puncheon. At 0.7 mile you come to a beaver dam, then hike uphill through a mixed hardand softwood forest. At 1.1 miles you pass by an old farm site with apple trees, a stone wall, and several foundations. Hike through an overgrown pasture, and continue through a birch stand. Cross the gated, gravel USFS Road–FR 341 at 1.3 miles. Make a note of this junction since you will be completing your return loop along this road.

Beyond the road, the trail ascends,

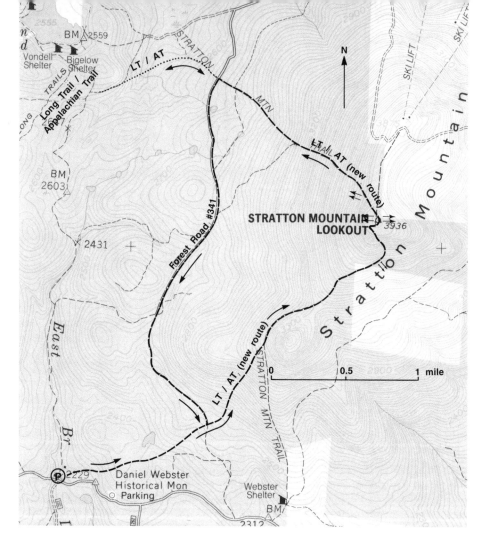

crosses a brook, and passes by several old logging roads. The trail gets steeper and reaches a shelf at 1.7 miles. Continue your steep ascent over uneven rocks up the ridge through a mixed hardwood forest with numerous birches. At 2.5 miles you intersect the old "Stratton Mountain Trail."

In the mid-1980s, Vermont's congressional delegation worked to obtain federal monies for acquisition of the western slope of Stratton Mountain. They were successful, but the Gramm-Rudman-Hollings deficit-reduction law delayed the funds. In

1985, The Nature Conservancy acquired 12,000 acres, including the summit, and held it in trust until the Forest Service received the allocated money. In 1986, after years of negotiation with the property owner, International Paper Company, the USFS obtained funding to finalize the purchase. The relocation, which involved 8.7 miles of new trail, was completed in 1989.

Continue your hike parallel to the ridgeline as the trail becomes less steep. Climb again along several switchbacks, pass among higher-elevation spruce and birch, and come to a view at 2.75

Mount Snow and Somerset Reservoir from Stratton Mountain

miles of Somerset Reservoir and Mount Snow. Beyond the overlook, ascend past a piped spring on your left. You now hike through primarily balsam fir trees along several switchbacks until you reach the fire tower at 3.4 miles.

Stratton Mountain was one of the earliest fire-tower sites in Vermont. A steel tower was constructed in 1914. In the early 1930s, a new cabin and a steel lookout tower were built by the Civilian Conservation Corps. This tower, abandoned as a fire tower around 1980, was repainted and repaired by the USFS in 1988. The only tower remaining on USFS Vermont lands, it was nominated to the National Register of Historic Places in 1989.

A ranger-naturalist, supported by the Green Mountain Club, Appalachian Trail Conference, and Green Moun-tain National Forest, is stationed on the summit during hiking season. No camping is permitted on the summit.

From the tower you can enjoy spec-tacular views: to the south, Somerset Reservoir and Mount Snow; to the southwest, Glastenbury Mountain; to the west, Mount Equinox and the Taconic Range; to the northeast, Mount Ascutney; and, to the south-east, Mount Monadnock. Unless you decide to take the shorter 6.8-mile route back down the same trail to your car, continue north on the LT/AT along the summit ridge and begin to descend. At 3.5 miles you reach an overlook of Stratton Pond with Mount Equinox in the distance. In the next section, the trail utilizes stone steps, water bars, and turnpiking to cross a wet area.

At 4.0 miles you steeply descend over rocks and roots in the trail and begin a series of long switchbacks through a softwood forest. As the trail passes through mixed hardwoods, you continue your descent and cross a small brook at 4.7 miles. The trail soon intersects several old logging roads, steeply descends for a short distance, and crosses a wet area on puncheon.

After a more moderate descent, you reach the gravel FR 341 at 5.1 miles. The LT/AT goes 1 mile straight ahead to Stratton Pond. You turn left and follow the USFS road to the LT/AT intersection (at 7.6 miles), which you passed at the beginning of your hike. Hike the LT/AT south back down the trail to your car at 9 miles.

7

Bald Mountain

Total distance: 3.5-mile loop

Hiking time: 3 hours

Vertical rise: 1100 feet

Rating: Moderate ascent/strenuous descent

Map: USGS 15' Saxtons River

Bald Mountain, located in Townshend State Forest, offers excellent views of the surrounding area. The Forest is located next to Townshend State Park where you can swim and picnic before or after your hike. On your way to the trail you pass the Scott Covered Bridge, which spans the West River. The bridge, built in 1870, is 165.7 feet long—the longest single-span covered bridge in Vermont.

How to Get There

To reach the Townshend State Forest, drive 2.0 miles north of Townshend Village on VT 30 to the Townshend Dam. Turn left (west), and cross the spillway on a narrow bridge. Just past the dam and recreation access (0.0), the road reaches a T at 0.2 mile. Turn left and pass the Scott Covered Bridge at 0.8 mile. Bear right at the bridge, and continue parallel to the West River until you reach the Park entrance at 1.4 miles. Parking is available in a small lot just before the Park building. Walk to the building, where a day-use fee is charged.

The Trail

Begin your hike across the road, to the right of the park building. Descend on a short spur trail to campsite #25, where the trailhead is marked with a sign and very large blue blazes. Take the trail over a brook on a pole bridge, turn left, and follow the brook along an old road. Take time to enjoy the brook's pretty cascades and pools. The road climbs a steep bank away from the brook but soon returns to cross the brook near a property line and an old bridge abutment. The trail bears left at an old road junction and ascends away from the brook. At 0.6 mile the trail bears right to avoid a logging area, then parallels and crosses a logging road. Ascend along the hillside, covered with small boulders, into an open softwood forest. The trail bears right and continues on easy grades through several wet areas.

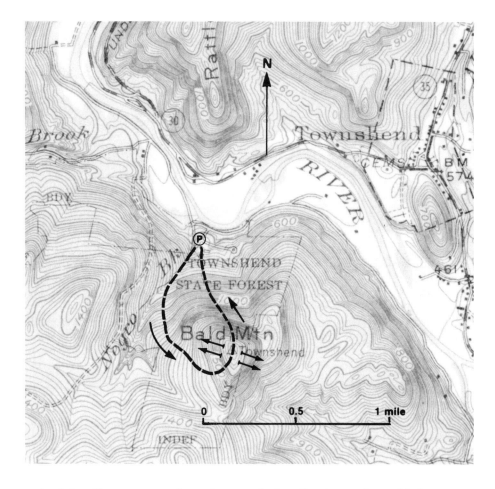

At 1.1 miles you pass by a large boulder and cross a brook. An old road intersects the trail, which now follows the brook bed. Bear left off the old brook bed and enter an alder swamp. The trail begins to ascend along the hillside, which resembles an overgrown, rocky old pasture. Look for numerous oak trees. Continue on the steep but quite open trail to the 1680-foot summit at 1.7 miles. A sign directs you to a southern view of Mount Monadnock in New Hampshire and the West River valley below you. The northern view includes Stratton and Bromley Mountains. Look for foundation footings of an old fire tower (between the two overlooks). A fire station was established on Bald Mountain in 1912. A steel tower was built on the summit in the early 1930s, but the tower was transferred to Mount Olga (see Hike 2).

From the summit, take the blue-blazed trail to the right of the northern overlook. You enter the woods and rapidly descend through softwoods. Watch your footing in this difficult section. At 2.0 miles the trail bears right to avoid an eroded area and begins a steep sidehill traverse on a very narrow trail. Occasional views are pos-

Glacial erratic

sible of Townshend Reservoir below as the trail continues its descent and crosses a small brook. At 2.8 miles the trail bears left again, descends steeply, and then continues gently downhill through a nice maple grove lined with ferns. Another steep descent takes you to 3.3 miles, where the downgrade eases up; eventually you reach the campground road near a huge tree stump at campsite #6. Follow this road back to the parking lot at 3.5 miles.

8

Prospect Rock (Manchester)

Total distance: *3 miles*

Hiking time: *2½ hours*

Vertical rise: *1100 feet*

Rating: *Strenuous*

Map: *USGS 7.5' Manchester*

Newt

This popular trail up Prospect Rock offers views of the Lye Brook Wilderness Area, Mount Equinox and Manchester Center.

How to Get There
Begin at the junction of VT 11/VT 30 and US 7 (0.0) about 1 mile east of Manchester. Drive east on VT 11/VT 30 for 0.5 mile to the junction of the East Manchester Road on your right. Take a right on East Manchester Road and after about 150 feet turn left onto Rootville Road. Follow it 0.5 mile to the white water tower on your right and a small gravel driveway and house. There is parking for five cars near the water tower at 1.05 miles, just before the "No Parking" signs. Do not block the road, and do not park near or drive past the signs.

The Trail
Begin your hike up unmaintained "Old Rootville Road" to a "Green Mountain National Forest" signboard on your right. Continue on the moderately graded old road up the side of the mountain, and listen to the brook flowing on your right. You pass a spur trail, the small brook comes into view on your right, and the old road as-

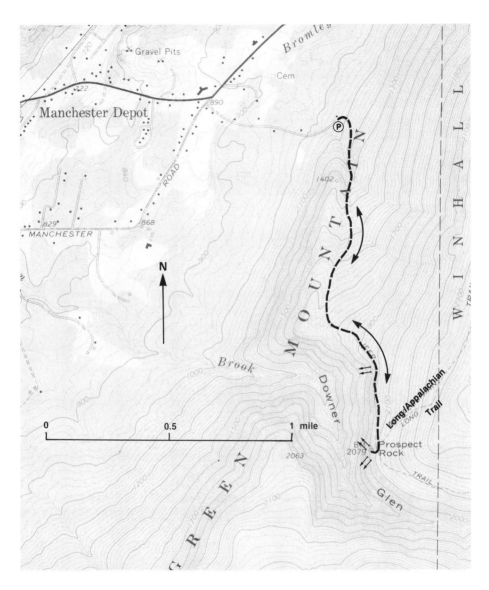

cends more steeply up the mountain.

This hike is wonderful in the fall because of the many different trees: white and yellow birch, maple, oak, and spruce. At 0.3 mile the road crosses the brook on an old culvert and is soon met by another small brook on your right. Continue to crisscross the brook until you reach a spring box on your left, where the brook turns to the left away from the road. After climbing to another spring at 0.8 mile, leave the sound of the brooks behind and enjoy a deep quiet interrupted only by birds and chipmunks.

The old road soon levels off and passes through a beautiful birch stand filled with sunlight—on days when clouds don't intercede. The trail eventually starts climbing again with a steep drop-off to your right and views of Downer Glen. At this point, the road is carved out of the side of the mountain and levels off before climbing on easier grades. Manchester Center and Mount Equinox can be seen through the trees.

At 1.5 miles you reach a junction where the white-blazed Long Trail branches off to your left and goes north to Spruce Peak and Bromley Mountain. Continue straight a few more feet on the old road to a spur trail on your right, which leads about 200 feet west to Prospect Rock.

From the Rock, high above Downer Glen, you can see the highway and Manchester Center. To the northwest, up the valley, is Dorset. Mount Aeolus is to the right of the valley and Mount Equinox, with its four windmills on the left of its summit, can be seen to the left of the valley.

After enjoying the views, return along the same trails to your car.

9

Antone Mountain

Total distance: 5 miles

Hiking time: 3 hours

Vertical rise: 890 feet

Rating: Moderate

Map: USGS 7.5' Pawlet

This hike follows only some of the 26 miles of trails at the Merck Forest and Farmland Center, a nonprofit outdoor educational facility that also contains a small diversified farm, fields, hardwood forests, and several small ponds and streams. It offers a variety of educational programs, including astronomy, forest management, wildflower and bird identification, and low-impact camping.

How to Get There

The center can be reached from the junction of VT 315 and VT 30 in East Rupert (0.0). Take VT 315 west 2.4 miles to the height-of-land and a Merck Forest sign on your left. Turn left on the dirt road and continue to a gate and a 10-car parking area at 2.9 miles. A signboard at the gate includes area rules (no mountain bikes; no unleashed dogs) as well as trail maps that are available with a donation to help cover the center's expenses.

The Trail

The unblazed trail, which follows old roads, starts from the gate. Follow the dirt road on level grades until you reach a field on your right. The caretaker's cabin, as well as cabins for overnight use, are on your left. At the road fork ahead there are picnic tables, a barn, and a visitors center. Take time to visit the center's interesting exhibits on area wildlife and forests.

Continue your hike on the Old Towne Road to the right at the fork. This road, the first one in Merck Forest, was built by Ebenezer Smith in 1781 to provide access between his home on the mountain and the town highway. The most recent roads are used for logging and sugaring, which help support the educational center. Old Towne Road passes several fields, descends for a short distance, and then ascends on easy grades. Enjoy the nice views to the north and northwest of New York's Adirondack Mountains.

Stay on Old Towne Road through

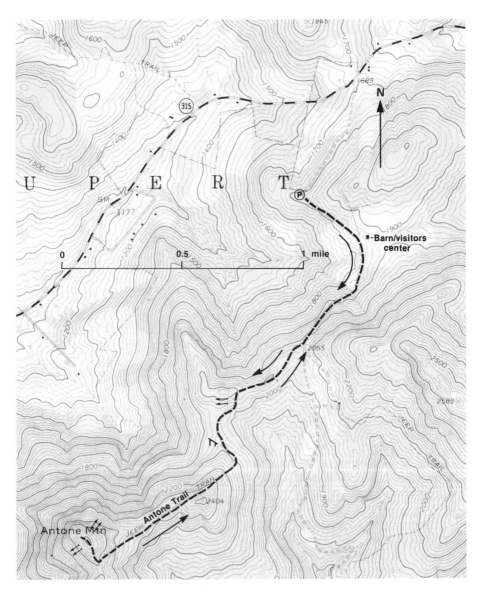

the Gallop Road intersection on your left and then the Old McCormick Road intersection on your right at 0.5 mile. Hike up a short, steep grade, and pass a small clearing on your right as the road levels again. Make a left turn, and come to a well-marked junction with Lodge Road on your left and Mount Antone Road on your right. Turn right on Mount Antone Road along easy grades on top of the ridge, and then descend to Clark's Clearing at 1.3 miles. You pass the McCormick Road junction on your right and a small lean-to for firewood on your left. Look for berry bushes in two small clearings, where you can feast on ripe berries in late July while enjoying views of Antone Mountain.

Follow the trail into the woods until you come to an overnight shelter and trail intersection. The Clark's Clearing Road bears left and a spur trail bears right. Continue to the south on the Mount Antone Road up a steep grade to the top of the ridge. The road levels and starts an easy, winding descent. At 1.9 miles you reach the Wade Lot Road junction on your left. Hike past the Lookout Road junction, again on your left, and climb the mountainside on moderate grades past the Beebe Pond Trail and Masters Mountain Trail junction. The Mount Antone Trail continues up a steep grade to the 2610-foot summit at 2.5 miles. There are views to the east and northeast of the visitor center's barn, Dorset Peak, Woodlawn Mountain, and the Pawlet area. A trail beyond the summit leads downhill to another lookout, with good views of the Adirondack Mountains, eastern New York, and the Rupert and Pawlet areas.

After enjoying the views, hike back to the summit and down the trail to the parking area at 5.0 miles.

10

Griffith Lake and Baker Peak

Total distance: 8.9 miles

Hiking time: 5 hours

Vertical rise: 2340 feet

Rating: Strenuous

Map: GMNF Wallingford NW

The first 3.5 miles of this strenuous hike follow the Lake Trail over an old road that was once a carriage road to the Griffith Lake House, a clubhouse near the summit of Baker Peak owned by Silas L. Griffith. The foundation of the house can still be seen on the west shore of the lake. Silas Griffith, Vermont's first millionaire, lived in Danby and operated a sawmill that became known as the town of Griffith.

How to Get There
Drive 2.2 miles south of Danby (0.0) on US 7 to a small, unmarked road on the left (east) side of US 7. Turn left on the road and cross a set of railroad tracks. The road passes a small cemetery on the right and at 2.7 miles reaches a small parking lot for five to six cars on the left.

The Trail
Your pathway starts at the right rear corner of the lot and ascends on easy grades. You soon cross a brook, hike parallel to the brook, and cross two smaller brooks. At 0.75 mile the old roadway widens through a hemlock grove but quickly narrows and begins a sweeping switchback to your left, until you reach a United States Forest Service (USFS) "No Vehicles" sign. Continue climbing past a steep ledge on your right. (Imagine the labor required to construct the old road.) At 1.6 miles you cross a rock slab on a narrow bridge. Look below in the rock for the metal pins that once held the carriage road bridge in place. A notch in the mountain ridge is visible ahead as the trail swings right. The trail gets steeper as you follow along McGinn Brook flowing out of the valley. At 2.0 miles you reach the junction of the Baker Peak Trail, on which you will return.

The Lake Trail bears right, continues upstream on easy grades, and crosses a brook as the trail becomes quite wet and rocky. Numerous small

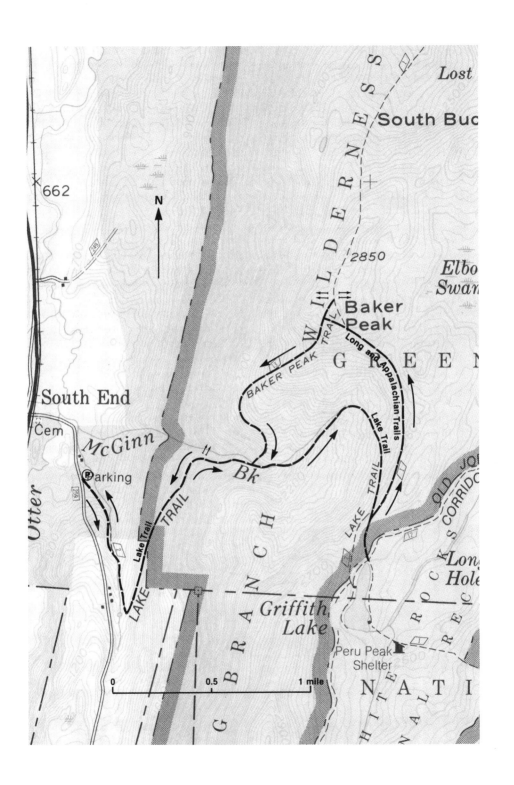

brooks cross the trail in this section. The trail bears right into the woods to avoid a very wet part of the old roadway. You soon return to the old road and pass through a maple forest on easy grades. The trail leaves the road at an obscure junction, crests a small knob, and reaches the LT/AT junction at 3.5 miles

Turn right and follow the white-blazed LT/AT to Griffith Lake. A high, 16-acre mountain lake, Griffith Lake was originally called Buffum Pond. This warm-water lake averages 10 feet deep and, although stocked with brook trout, is not a particularly good fishing site. All camping at the lake is restricted to designated sites within 200 feet of the shore, and a small fee is charged for overnight use. A Green Mountain Club caretaker is stationed at the lake during hiking season.

After enjoying the lake, return to the trail junction at 3.7 miles, and follow the LT/AT north along a relatively level grade to Baker Peak. From the junction, hike up, down, and over wet areas on puncheon until you reach a large boulder. Continue over several rock shelves with occasional views along the birch-lined hillside. At 5.4 miles you reach the Baker Peak Trail Junction. Follow the LT/AT up the exposed rock slab to the summit. Be very careful of your footing along the slab. From the summit of Baker Peak you have great views of Dorset Peak directly across the valley, Mount Equinox and the Stratton Mountain fire tower to the south, and the Otter Creek meandering through the narrow US 7 valley below.

From the summit, return to the junction and steeply descend the ridge along the blue-blazed Baker Peak Trail. You quickly reach an overlook—called "Quarry View"—of the stone quarries on Dorset Peak. After enjoying the view, descend more gradually along a rock outcrop through mixed hardwoods. The trail soon bears right and begins a steep descent until you enter a fern-filled maple forest, where the trail levels slightly. The trail now resembles an old road. You begin to hear water as you reach the Lake Trail Junction at 6.9 miles.

Turn right, cross the brook, and return along the old carriage road to your car at 8.9 miles.

11

Little Rock Pond/ Green Mountain Trail

Total distance: 7-mile loop

Hiking time: 6–7 hours

Vertical rise: 960 feet

Rating: Moderately strenuous

Map: GMNF Wallingford NW and SW

This hike, which provides a nice variation for the usual "out-and-back" trail, allows you to enjoy both mountain trails and a beautiful pond. Leave a full day for this journey to give yourself adequate time to enjoy the pond, as well as some wonderful views.

How to Get There
To reach the trail, take US 7 to its junction (0.0) with United States Forest Service (USFS) Road–FR 10 (near the towns of Danby and Mount Tabor). Turn east on FR 10, also called the Danby-Landgrove Road, cross the railroad tracks, and go by the USFS Mount Tabor Work Center Sign. Follow the road uphill to a sign at 0.9

mile that indicates you have entered the White Rocks National Recreational Area. At 2.7 miles you reach Big Branch Overlook. The road turns to dirt at 3.0 miles. You soon cross a bridge and reach the Long Trail parking area at 3.2 miles, where there is space for approximately 20 cars.

The Trail
Cross the road and follow the white-blazed Long Trail north to Little Rock Pond. The sign post at the trailhead indicates a distance of 2 miles to the pond, your first stop on this hike. The beginning of this trail, which starts as a gradual climb, is strewn with bricks and black soot from an old charcoal kiln. Enter some mixed hardwoods and start to leave the brook behind. You follow an old roadway parallel to the brook on your left and soon cross the brook on a steel I-beam bridge at 0.6 mile.

The trail swings right after the bridge and continues to follow, then crosses, the brook. By 1.0 mile the brook is considerably smaller as you cross a wet area on puncheon. The trail then switches from a roadway into a more "rugged" path with numerous slippery wet areas, so be sure to watch

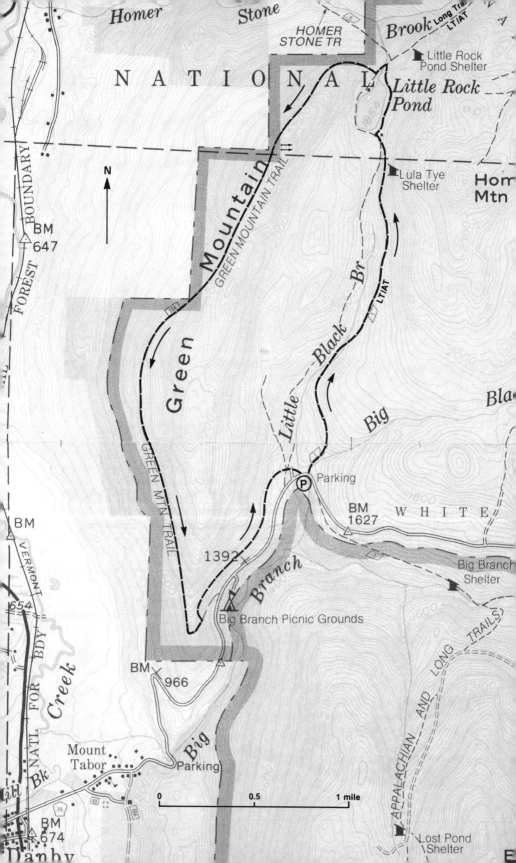

Mallards

your step. At 1.8 miles you reach a spur trail on your right that goes to the Lula Tye Shelter. In 1972 members of the Student Conservation Association moved this shelter from Little Rock Pond to its current location to reduce hiker impact on the pond area. The shelter is named in memory of the woman who served as Green Mountain Club corresponding secretary from 1926 to 1955.

A sign at this junction says the pond is 0.2 mile farther along the Long Trail. The trail becomes very rocky during this next section, so be careful of your footing until you reach the south end of the pond at 2.0 miles.

Little Rock Pond, up to 60 feet deep in places, is one of the most popular day- and overnight-use areas on the Long Trail. A good fishing spot, the pond is annually stocked with brook trout. Beavers frequent the area, and moose have occasionally been sighted along the pond shore. Careful management is required to preserve the area's natural beauty and fragile shoreline environment. Due to the area's popularity, a Green Mountain Club caretaker is stationed at the site during the hiking season.

A signboard points out the trails around the pond and the campsites. As you follow the Long Trail around the pond, you soon cross a piped spring. At 2.4 miles you reach the north end of the pond. Continue north and cross a brook to the junction of the Green Mountain Trail and the Little Rock Pond Loop. The Long Trail continues straight ahead, but you turn left on the pond loop and Green Mountain Trail. A sign indicates a distance of 0.9 mile to the pond lookout and 4.5 miles back to the parking lot.

Ascend the trail to "Loop Junction" at 2.5 miles and turn right, away from the pond, on the blue-blazed Green

Mountain Trail. Switchback up the ridge, and climb up the edge of a pointed rock outcrop. Occasional views along the trail remind you how far you have climbed above the pond. At 3.0 miles you reach a ledge with views down to the pond. Return to a wooded ridge walk, climb over a steep rock face, and reach the "Pond View" junction. Hike straight ahead for 100 yards to spectacular views of the pond and valley below.

From the junction, the trail takes a sharp right into a spruce forest, with minor ascents and switchbacks. Pass through a series of rock shelves and, on the left at 3.7 miles, you can take a short spur trail to a nice view. Back on the main trail, which now resembles an old road, descend through some mixed hardwoods. The trail is quite wide in this section. The end of the first major descent is reached at 4.5 miles, where you turn left and continue through mature hardwoods. Be careful to watch for blazes in this area. Continue your descent until you cross a brook at 5.2 miles and enter a much younger hardwood forest. The trail climbs again, then levels off. You soon reach a very unusual old road cut out of the hillside. Enjoy views of the valley along the road. As you cross a rock slide, take time to notice that the area uphill is predominantly hardwood, while the valley below is all softwood; the road forms the dividing line. The trail then swings around the edge of the ridge, and you begin to hear Big Branch Brook.

At 6.4 miles you reach another trail junction, where you turn left to return to your car. The trail straight ahead leads to another parking lot and FR 10. As you turn left and return to the woods, you pass among some beech trees and ascend along an old road. At the bottom of the hill you begin to see FR 10 on the right as your cross a wet overgrown area parallel to it. At 7.0 miles you cross a gravel road, pass through another wet overgrown area, and descend to the road. Turn left and return to the parking lot.

12

White Rocks/Ice Beds Trail

Total distance: 2 miles

Hiking time: 1½ hours

Vertical rise: 460 feet

Rating: Easy

Map: GMNF Wallingford NW

This relatively easy hike offers wonderful views of the White Rocks Cliff and the "Ice Beds," where ice, formed beneath the rocks during the previous winter, chills a meltwater stream.

How to Get There

Drive east on VT 140 from the VT 140/US 7 junction in Wallingford (0.0) to Sugarhill Road at 2.2 miles. Turn right, drive about 150 yards on Sugarhill Road, and turn right on United States Forest Service (USFS) Road–FR 52. Continue to the White Rocks Picnic Area at 2.8 miles. The picnic area has ample parking for 30 cars, along with picnic facilities and outhouses. (Note: The picnic area is also the trailhead for a different trail—

the Keewaydin Trail—leading 0.8 mile to the Long Trail.)

The Trail

Near the entrance to the picnic area is a trailhead sign for the blue-blazed Ice Beds Trail. You immediately pass through a small wet area on bridges and turnpiking. Large rock outcrops appear on your left, and boulders dot the area as you hike up the hillside. The trail swings to your right and climbs through boulders and softwoods. Hike along a switchback, then ascend more steeply to a trail junction at 0.3 mile.

From this point, the White Rocks Trail leads left to a spectacular view of the White Rocks Cliff and the Otter Creek valley to the southwest. A talc mine in South Wallingford on US 7 is also visible.

Because peregrine falcons have returned to the area and may be nesting on the cliffs, the White Rocks Trail may be closed during their nesting season because these beautiful endangered birds are easily disturbed from above. Please obey all posted signs, and refer to the introduction for more information about the falcons.

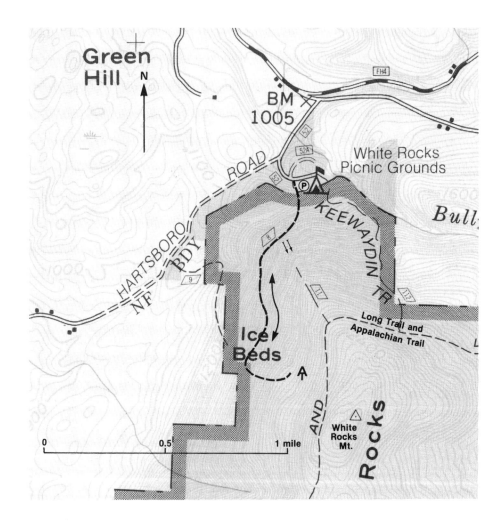

Return to the junction, and continue uphill along the Ice Beds Trail. Enjoy the good view back to White Rocks before you hike behind the ridge and have only limited views to the north. The trail is quite rocky in this section, so watch your step. The trail soon levels before descending toward, then away from, the base of White Rocks Cliff. At the double blaze, turn right and begin a rocky descent. Follow the blazes along a series of small switchbacks as the trail becomes less steep and more wooded. You begin to hear a brook to your left, and the air feels cool and damp.

After descending a few steps, you reach a junction with an old road, where you go left and downhill. Cross a brook on a small bridge, and follow along the valley floor. You soon cross the brook again, ascend slightly, and at 1.0 mile reach the Ice Beds, where the brook you have been following emerges from the base of the White Rocks Slide.

White Rocks Mountain and Cliffs

The USFS sign at the location reads:

A shattering of cheshire quartzite rock probably occurred during the ice age to create this rock slide. During the winter, ice and snow accumulate in the depths of the rock crevices. A continual downdraft of cold air in the shaded canyon helps preserve the ice and snow during the summer. The stream flowing from the rocks is fed by the melting ice. This keeps the water temperature at approximately 40 degrees throughout the summer.

After enjoying this cool, refreshing retreat (especially on a hot summer day!), hike back via the same trail to the picnic area.

13

Little Rock Pond and Clarendon Gorge

Total distance: 14.4 miles

Hiking time: 2 days, 1 night

Vertical rise: 2775 feet

Rating: Day 1—moderate; Day 2—easy

Maps: GMNF Wallingford SW and NW, USGS 7.5' Rutland

This enjoyable hike along the Long Trail is appropriate for even a novice backpacker. The trail crosses valleys, passes mountain ponds, follows ridgelines, crests mountains, and concludes across a suspension bridge over Clarendon Gorge. There are ample opportunities both days for swimming as well as numerous scenic vistas.

The suspension bridge over the gorge was built in 1974. For several years, until the mid-1950s, an old timber bridge spanned the gorge, but it was removed when it decayed and became unsafe. The Green Mountain Club's Killington Section planned a new bridge in 1955 and finally completed construction in the spring of 1957. The bridge held strong until the flood of 1973 washed it away. Four days later, tragedy struck when 17-year-old Robert Brugmann, attempting to cross the still-swollen river on a fallen tree, slipped, fell into the stream, and drowned.

A subsequent relocation made such a long detour to reach the bridge in East Clarendon that the Green Mountain Club planned a new bridge. With a design from GMC member Allan St. Peter, major technical assistance from the Vermont Department of Highways, and memorial gifts from Robert Brugmann's family and friends, construction started in the spring of 1974. The bridge cost almost $8000, quite a difference from the $700 bridge constructed in 1957! Highway engineers, United States Forest Service personnel, and Green Mountain Club volunteers worked together during various steps along the way to complete the bridge in July 1974.

The first day, you hike past Little Rock Pond and over White Rocks Mountain to Greenwall Shelter, where you spend the night. Little Rock Pond, up to 60 feet deep in places, is one of the most popular day-use areas and the highest overnight-use area on the Long Trail. The pond is a good fishing spot and annually stocked with

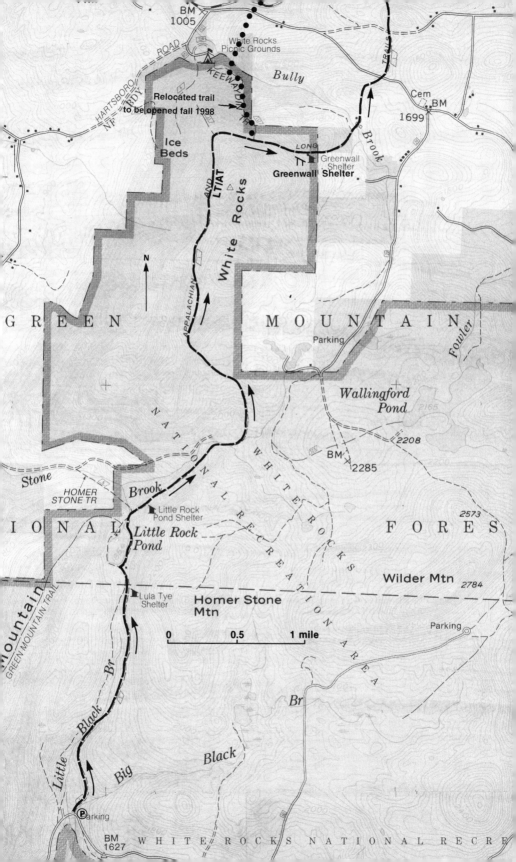

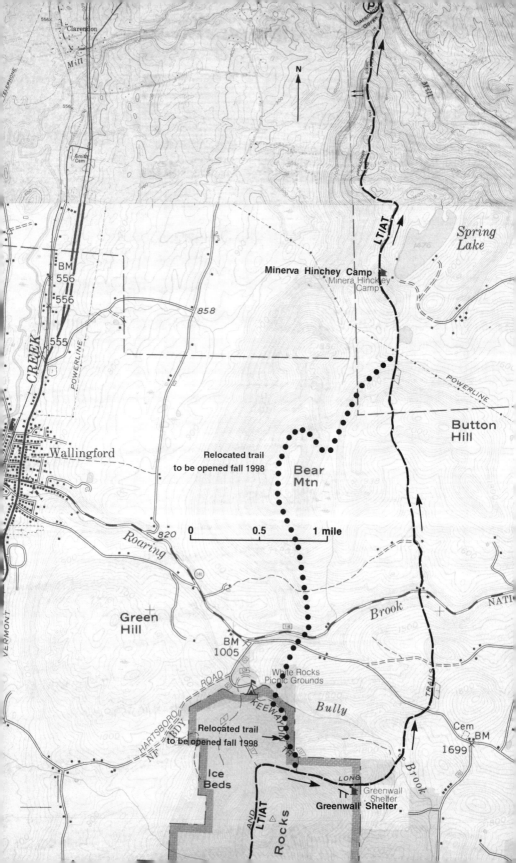

brook trout. Beavers frequent the area, and moose have occasionally been sighted along the pond shore. Careful management is required to preserve the area's natural beauty and fragile shoreline environment. Due to the area's high use, a Green Mountain Club caretaker is stationed at the site during the hiking season. An overnight-use fee is charged.

The second day, you cross VT 140, hike through overgrown farmlands and pastures, continue along a rocky ridge, and finish across Clarendon Gorge on the suspension bridge.

How to Get There

Spot a car on the south side of VT 103 at the Clarendon Gorge parking area, 2.1 miles east of the US 7 and VT 103 junction, and approximately 5.0 miles south of Rutland. Avoid the temptation to explore the gorge so that it remains the reward at the end of your journey. Vandalism can be a problem at this parking area; see the introduction for specific precautions to follow.

To reach the trail where you begin your journey, take US 7 to Danby, where a sign points east to Mount Tabor and United States Forest Service (USFS) Road–FR 10. Turn east on FR 10 and drive 3.5 miles to the Long Trail Parking Area at Big Black Branch. Because this trailhead is popular with hikers traveling to Little Rock Pond, there is an outhouse as well as a trailhead information board.

The Trail

Day One

Total distance: 7.2 miles

Hiking time: 4½ to 5 hours

Vertical rise: 1275 feet

Begin your hike over easy terrain along the Little Black Branch on an old road.

At 0.6 mile you cross the brook on a single I-beam bridge and bear right along the brook. Notice that the brook gets smaller as you cross it again. Continue up the hillside, occasionally on puncheon. At 1.8 miles you reach a spur trail on the right to Lula Tye Shelter, which was moved from Little Rock Pond to this location in 1972 to reduce hiker impact on the pond area. The shelter is named in memory of the woman who served as Green Mountain Club corresponding secretary from 1926 to 1955.

Continue on the Long Trail until you approach the end of Little Rock Pond, where a signboard explains the pond ecology and area trails. Bear right and come to a tenting area on a knoll behind the tent of the Green Mountain Club caretaker, who is stationed at the site during the hiking season. Nestled among the mountains at an elevation of 1854 feet, Little Rock Pond is a scenic place to swim, rest, and cool off. An overnight-use fee is charged.

Hike along the shore among dense conifers to the pond outlet at 2.4 miles, where the Green Mountain Trail and, just after, the Homer Stone Brook Trail bear left. Continue straight ahead to a spur trail on the right to Little Rock Pond Shelter. Built by the USFS in 1962, the shelter was moved in 1972 from its former location on the pond's small island.

From the shelter, the Long Trail passes through an old clearing on easy grades and crosses Homer Stone Brook and the old South Wallingford/Wallingford Pond Road at 3.6 miles. You now begin a sometimes steep and rocky ascent up White Rocks Mountain through dense softwoods and pass just west of the summit at 5.6 miles. An old blue-blazed side trail on the left, which leads to a fantastic view from the top of White Rocks Cliff, may be closed if peregrine falcons are nesting on the cliffs. If the area is posted, please obey the signs.

Descend on the LT to the Keewaydin Trail junction at 6.7 miles. You continue following the Long Trail as you descend to Greenwall Shelter, where you end your day at 7.2 miles. The shelter, a frame lean-to for eight, was also built by the USFS in 1962. There are a few tenting sites behind the shelter. A blue-blazed trail leads 600 feet northeast to a spring, which may fail in very dry weather.

Day Two

Total distance: 7.2 miles

Hiking time: 4½ to 5 hours

Vertical rise: 1500 feet

Descend from the shelter through an overgrown pasture (be prepared for wet legs), and come to Sugar Hill Road at 0.6 mile. Turn left and follow the road to the junction of FR 19. Cross the road and enter the woods. At 0.9 mile you cross the Roaring Brook and reach VT 140 across a bridge. Turn right on and ascend a gravel road until the trail turns right on an old farm road at 2.4 miles.

After a sharp left turn, you soon return to the woods and begin a steep ascent to the summit of Button Hill at 3.5 miles. The summit is marked by a wooden sign on a tree. Descend from the summit, cross a power line, and reach a short, unmarked spur trail to the Minerva Hinchey Shelter at 4.6 miles. Minerva Hinchey was the Green Mountain Club corresponding secre-

tary for 22 years. The shelter is a nice spot to eat lunch and rest before the final leg of your journey.

Continue your hike on the Long Trail up a hardwood ridge and down to Spring Lake Clearing. This meadow is periodically cleared in the spring through prescribed burns by the USFS, Green Mountain Club, and others. By burning at appropriate and safe times, the growth of grasses and ferns is encouraged while brush and trees are discouraged. This clearing is a National Park Service pilot project to maintain the view and foster wildlife.

Hike along the ridge until you reach Airport Lookout at 6.2 miles, with a good western view of the Otter Creek valley, Rutland, and the Taconic Range. Descend from the outcrop, cross a roadway, and continue down until you reach the Mill River and Clarendon Gorge at 7.1 miles. Cross the gorge on the suspension bridge. As you look down into the deep gorge, picture the river during floods, when the water can rise high enough to touch the bridge! After dropping off your gear at your car, you may wish to further explore and enjoy this scenic area and popular swimming hole.

Note: The Long Trail and Appalachian Trails will be relocated in 1998 to the west of the current route between White Rocks Mountain and Minerva Hinchey Shelter. Greenwall Shelter will be accessible via a short spur trail. The new route is shown on the maps, but not reflected in the text. The current Long Trail/Appalachian Trail between Greenwall Shelter and the Powerline Crossing will be closed in Fall 1998.

14

Mount Ascutney

Total distance: 6 miles

Hiking time: 4½ hours

Vertical rise: 2250 feet

Rating: Strenuous

Map: USGS 7.5' Mount Ascutney

Lady's-slipper

Mount Ascutney is an unusual quartz monadnock (a hill or mountain of resistant rock) located near Windsor. The mountain's quartz syenite rock has withstood the erosion and glaciation that has worn away the softer rocks of the surrounding piedmont peneplain, an area near the foot of a mountain that has been almost reduced to a plain by erosion.

The first trail on Mount Ascutney was opened in 1825. The mountain derives its name from the Abenaki words *Cas-Cad-Nac*, meaning "mountain of the rocky summit." In 1883, a summer-long forest fire burned away stretches of trail on the mountain. Great boulders lined the trails, and charred tree trunks and ash were everywhere. The Ascutney Mountain Association was formed in 1903 to relocate many of the damaged trails, rebuild the destroyed hut on top of the mountain, and perpetually maintain the hut and trails.

In 1920, a ranger cabin and tower were constructed on the mountain. Around 1940, the Civilian Conservation Corps (CCC) built a new steel tower, which was abandoned as a fire tower in the 1950s. The tower remained standing until the mid-1980s.

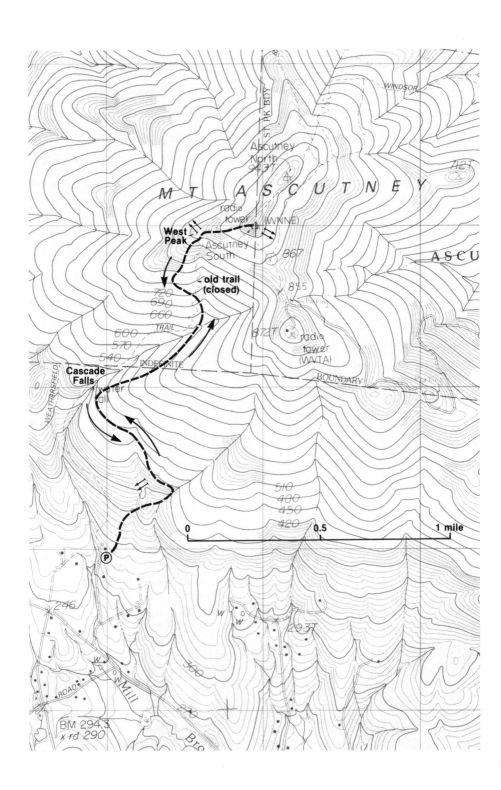

The building of a road in 1934 by the CCC, as well as the Great Hurricane of 1938, created so much debris and so many trail problems that little maintenance was done on the trails until 1966. In that year the Herbert Ogdens (junior and senior) located, cleared, blazed, signed, measured, and mapped the Windsor Trail. In 1967, the Ascutney Trails Association was formed to continue their work; it still maintains the trails on the mountain.

Because of several summit antennas, the summit is not as interesting as the west peak, which is more secluded and used as a hang glider launching site.

How to Get There

Take exit 8 (Ascutney) off I-91 to VT 131 west (0.0). Drive 3.3 miles to Cascade Falls Road, and turn right (north). Bear left at the fork, and continue to a right turn at 3.6 miles. Drive up the short steep hill to the 15-car parking lot and the Ascutney State Park information board. The trailhead and parking area were built in 1989 by the state of Vermont and the Ascutney Trails Association.

The Trail

From the information board at the left rear end of the parking lot, take the blue-blazed Weathersfield Trail, which ascends some small log stairs and enters the woods. Several property stakes line the trail. Swing right along easy grades and cross a small brook. The trail becomes rocky, ascends a steep gully along switchbacks, and crosses over Little Cascade Falls. Turn left, continue your ascent through a deep rock cleft, and hike out the other side on rock and log steps. Now on easier grades, pass several overlooks at 0.6 mile. The trail intersects an old road and enters a

softwood forest. Descend to Cascade Falls, then turn right, and ascend along the falls.

The geology of Crystal Cascade appears to be unique in Vermont. It is a rare example of a ring dike, formed by the upward flow of magma in a somewhat circular fissure. The molten rock made its way through overlying sedimentary rocks; however, the fledgling volcano lacked the thrust necessary to reach the surface, and all the magma cooled off underground. Subsequent erosion and glaciation wore away much of the overlying bedrock, exposing the igneous edge of the ring dike. The rocks at the border of the newly formed pluton (any body of igneous rock solidified far below the earth's surface) were metamorphosed by the extreme heat of the magma. This contact zone is clearly visible at the base of Crystal Cascade, where a second bedrock shows as a gray mass. Evidence of the ring dike formation can also be found at the top of the Cascades. Chunks of the surrounding bedrock were constantly consumed by the magma as it moved upward. However, pieces that were only partially absorbed when the magma cooled are said to be visible in the flat outcrops above the cliff. The only other large example of a ring dike is in Norway, where they call it a *nordmarkite*.

At 1.3 miles the trail levels slightly, and you begin to see the Ascutney ridge line across the valley. After crossing the bottom of the valley and a brook, climb a small bank and turn right on an old roadway. You are now on the old Weathersfield Trail, which is blazed in white, so expect a combination of white and blue blazes to the summit. Continue on the roadway past several rock outcrops to Halfway Brooks at 1.7 miles. Turn left, and follow the sign's instructions to stay on the trail and not take shortcuts as you ascend the steep ridge. Erosion in this area is a serious problem that you can help control by staying on the trail. Still climbing, you pass exposed rock outcrops, where you can rest and enjoy the views. Swing right through some stunted birches, and return to the woods on easier grades.

At 2.3 miles make a sharp right turn at Gus's Lookout, a series of large rock outcrops with views of the valley and the summit ridge. The lookout was named for Augustus Aldrich, a hiker who died in 1974 on Mount Katahdin at age 86.

Return to the woods, pass a large boulder, and follow a switchback through a fern-filled white birch grove. Bear left to a trail junction. A spur to the left leads to the west peak with views to the east of the Connecticut River Valley and to the west of the Green Mountain Range. Continue straight from the trail junction for nice views to the north. The antennae-covered summit is reached at 2.9 miles by taking a right at the junction and ascending through overgrowth. When leaving the summit, be careful not to take the white-blazed trail, which leads to a parking lot at the top of the Ascutney Trail Road.

Return to the junction, and hike back down the trail to your car.

CENTRAL VERMONT

15

Okemo Mountain

Total distance: 5.8 miles

Hiking time: 4 hours

Vertical rise: 1900 feet

Rating: Moderate

Map: USGS 7.5' Ludlow and 7.5' Mount Holly

Okemo is a mountain of contrasts, with a ski area on one side and a wilderness hiking trail on the other. Built in the summers of 1991 to 1993 by the Youth Conservation Corps, this blue-blazed trail ascends 2.9 miles from the village of Healdville (named for its first postmaster) to the 3343-foot summit of Okemo Mountain. On the summit you will find a fire tower complete with a 360-degree view of the surrounding region. The mountain, the highest peak in town, was known as Ludlow Mountain until the development of the ski area.

How to Get There

From the junction of VT 140 and 103 in East Wallingford, follow VT 103 east until reaching the Station Road

at 6.5 miles. Turn right onto Station Road and follow it until reaching a grade crossing with the Green Mountain Railroad at the hamlet of Healdville at 7.2 miles. A signed parking lot with room for 10 cars is located just past the tracks on the left, at the former site of the Healdville Station. Be sure to check out the trailhead information board by the track crossing.

From the east, follow VT 103 west from the junction of VT 100/103 just north of Ludlow. Reach Station Road at 2.75 miles. Turn right onto Station Road to the railroad crossing at 3.5 miles and the trailhead parking lot.

The Trail

From the parking lot, follow the blue-blazed trail parallel to the railroad tracks, across a small bridge at 0.2 mile, and over several small brooks as you gently ascend. The mix of dense, small hardwoods that surrounds you is an indication of past logging in this area. Leave the logging road and brook you have been following, and ascend a small hill at 1.1 miles. The trail begins a series of switchbacks as the grade increases, and you pass glacial boulders and rock outcrops. At 1.5 miles

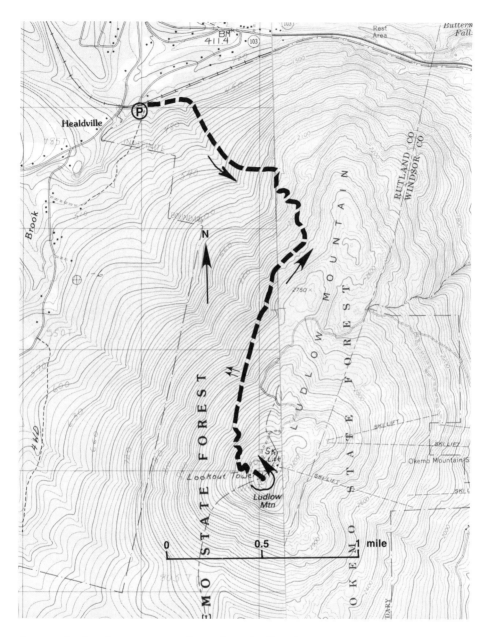

the grade levels as you reach a plateau. Notice how much more mature the forest is now.

Swing left at 1.8 miles, continue your ascent, and cross an old road until you reach a sign at 1.9 miles indicating you are 1 mile from the summit. Descend gradually, cross a rock-filled gully, and pass by rock outcrops as the trail gets steeper and you pass through a grove of white birch. At 2.3 miles you reach an overlook to

View from Okemo Mountain firetower

the east with VT 103 below you. Beyond the overlook ascend again as
the forest changes to spruce and fir
and the trail becomes rockier. At 2.8
miles take a sharp left turn through a
switchback to a northern view of
Killington Peak and Echo Lake, which
locals called Lake Tyson.

Isaac Tyson Jr., originally from
Baltimore, Maryland, discovered iron
in this region in 1835. He developed
the "Tyson Furnace" into what was
once one of the most productive iron
regions in New England.

After enjoying the view, continue
on the now level trail to an overgrown
area where you will find the chimney, foundation, and wood remains

of a forest ranger's cabin. Just beyond the cabin site, look for an arrow on a tree that points right to the
summit firetower. Follow the firetower trail, avoiding spur trails that
lead to the ski area. You reach the
tower, still complete with a roof, at
2.9 miles.

Be sure to enjoy the panoramic 360-
degree view of southern Vermont.
Below you is the Okemo Ski Area, east
is Mount Ascutney with its antennae,
north is Killington Peak, directly south
are Stratton and Bromley Mountains,
and southwest are Dorset Peak and
the Taconic Range. After resting and
enjoying the beautiful view, return
via the same trails to your car.

16

Pico Peak

Total distance: 5.4 miles

Hiking time: 3½ hours

Vertical rise: 1800 feet

Rating: Moderate

Map: USGS 7.5' Pico Peak

Pico Peak is a popular hike because of the short, steep trail that leads to an open summit with excellent views. The trail's proximity to a major road, however, means you will probably have plenty of company on your hike!

The Inn at the Long Trail, where your hike begins, is located near the site of the original Long Trail Lodge, the former headquarters of the GMC, which was built in the early 1920s with a gift from the Proctor family. The lodge was an intriguing structure—with a rock ledge wall, a huge stone fireplace, and the Long Trail passing through the building. At one point in the late 1930s, skiers could actually ski from an annex across the road directly to the Pico Peak ski tow. Although the Green Mountain Club survived the Great Depression in fairly good financial shape, the years of

World War II were not so easy. In 1955, after 30 years of ownership, the club needed additional funds and decided to sell the lodge. Unfortunately, the lodge was destroyed by fire in 1968.

In 1992, almost 40 years after the lodge was sold, the Green Mountain Club established permanent headquarters on Route 100 in Waterbury Center. Once again, Vermonters, visitors, club members, and volunteers have a comfortable and central place to gather for hiking and outdoor recreation information and events. The Green Mountain Club also opened the Marvin B. Gameroff Hiker Center, which in 1993 alone assisted over 3500 visitors and responded to tens of thousands of requests from around the country.

How to Get There

Take US 4 to the top of Sherburne Pass (about 9 miles east of Rutland). Park on the south side of the road, opposite the Inn at the Long Trail, where you will find parking for approximately 25 cars.

The Trail

Take the trail directly behind the parking lot. Walk south past the re-

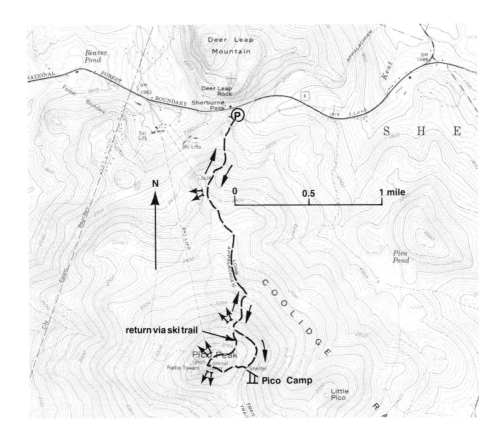

mains of two buildings until you reach a registration box where the white-blazed Long Trail bears right and begins to ascend. You will soon reach an old Killington Section sign that states that this section of the Long Trail is "dumpless." This sign was erected because hikers used to make a habit of burying their trash at a dump near the shelters. The sign now serves as a reminder of the Green Mountain Club policy: "Pack it in, pack it out!"

Following a moderate grade, you ascend onto a ridge and at 0.6 mile reach a spur trail to a view of Pico Ski Area. The noise you may hear is the alpine slide, which operates during the summer. Bear left and continue on easy grades. Enjoy occasional, al-though limited, views of the Pico ridge ahead. At 1.1 miles the trail becomes steeper and passes along Sink Hole Brook, a permanent stream that disappears into a sinkhole along the trail.

The trail eventually bears right and begins a sidehill traverse until it reaches a ski trail at 2.1 miles. The trail turns left and follows the ski trail uphill for about 50 yards, then turns left again and reenters the woods. This lookout, known as Pico Junction, provides views north to Deer Leap and Chittenden Reservoir. Make a special note of the junction location because you may choose to return to this junction via the ski trail.

After reentering the woods above the lookout, the trail is much rockier with a somewhat downhill pitch. Be careful to watch your footing in this section. At 2.5 miles you cross a spring and reach Pico Camp. This frame cabin, with bunk space for 12, was built for the Killington Section by the Long Trail Patrol in 1959. The camp is a good place to take a break before continuing to the summit of Pico.

Continue your hike behind Pico Camp following the blue-blazed Pico Peak Trail. The trail is very steep, but quite short—only 0.4 mile to the summit. After passing what looks like the summit (but isn't), bear left until you reach a ski trail/work road. Bear left again and cross to another ski trail. Continue on the blue-blazed trail to the 3957-foot summit of Pico at 2.9 miles.

The summit offers two extensive viewing points. From the ski trails to the north you can see US 4 below, Deer Leap Mountain and Kent Pond to the right, and to the left of Deer Leap, the Chittenden Reservoir and part of the Green Mountain range. Watch Deer Leap carefully—you may spot some rock climbers. Near the radio towers (please heed the "Keep Out" signs; the towers operate under very high voltage) is a southern view of Killington Peak, Little Killington, Mendon Peak, and Parker's Gore.

After enjoying the views, you have two return options to Pico Junction. You could return via the same route, or, to create a small loop, continue along the ski trail/work road a short distance and then bear right onto the "Summit Glade" ski trail (note the blue blazes on rocks). Descend via this ski trail to Pico Junction at 3.3 miles. From Pico Junction return via the Long Trail to the parking lot at 5.4 miles.

Note: The relocation of the Long Trail/ Appalachian Trail around Pico Peak in 1998/1999 will affect this hike. The route followed will no longer be the Long Trail/Appalachian Trail.

17

Deer Leap Mountain

Total distance: 2 miles

Hiking time: 1½ hours

Vertical rise: 700 feet

Rating: Easy

Map: USGS 7.5' Pico Peak

The Deer Leap Trail is a unique introductory day hike that includes portions of the Long and Appalachian Trails, as well as a side trail that leads to a spectacular view from the top of Deer Leap Cliffs. The cliffs are a popular climbing area, so be sure to look for rock climbers.

In southern Vermont, the Appalachian Trail coincides with the Long Trail from the Massachusetts border to "Maine Junction." From there the Appalachian Trail continues east through Vermont and across the White Mountains in New Hampshire to Maine. The Long Trail heads north to Canada.

Built by volunteers between 1921 and 1937, the Appalachian Trail extends 2100 miles from Springer Mountain in Georgia to Mount Katahdin in Maine. It was first proposed in 1921 by Benton MacKaye, a forester, author, and philosopher. On Stratton Mountain in Vermont, MacKaye conceived the idea of connecting the high peaks of the East after construction of the Long Trail had already begun. Today, over 80 local, state, and federal agencies; the Appalachian Trail Conference; local nonprofit trail groups such as the Green Mountain Club; individual volunteers; community groups; and more than 1000 private landowners—in 14 states—work together to maintain and preserve this valuable recreational resource.

How to Get There
Take US 4 to the top of Sherburne Pass (about 9 miles east of Rutland) and the Inn at Long Trail. The inn offers parking for eight cars (no overnight parking allowed). There is also space for 25 cars on the south side of US 4.

The Trail
Begin your hike on the north side of US 4, and follow the white-blazed Long Trail/Appalachian Trail over the first set of boulders. Be careful to avoid the Cliff Trail on your left, which has

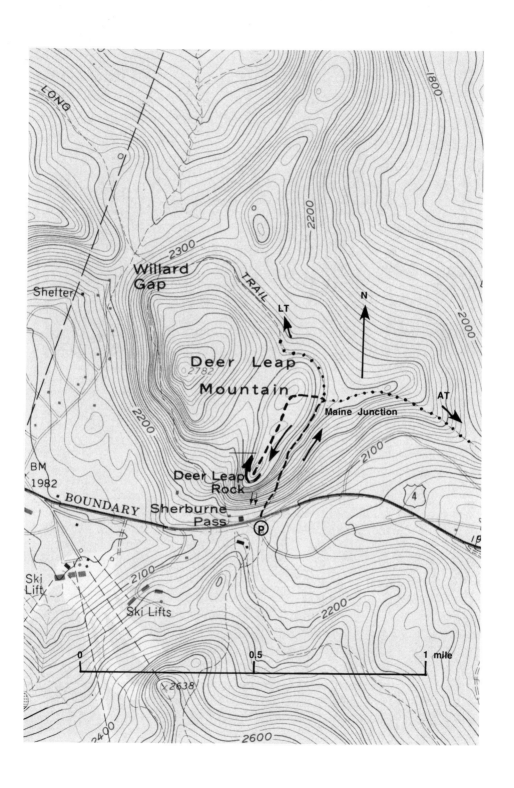

Pico Peak from Deer Leap

been closed and relocated due to severe erosion and safety concerns. You soon pass over more boulders. As you listen to traffic on US 4 below you in Sherburne Pass, you reach a steep rock face. The trail descends to your right to avoid this face, levels out, and then ascends until you reach "Maine Junction" at 0.5 mile. Be sure not to take a right turn, which would take you on the Appalachian Trail (also blazed in white) to Maine.

You continue straight ahead to the north on the white-blazed Long Trail and almost immediately reach the junction of the blue-blazed Deer Leap Overlook Trail. This trail was constructed by the United States Forest Service in 1994 to replace the eroded and unsafe Cliff Trail.

Turn left onto the Overlook Trail and ascend until you crest a series of small spruce fir knobs at 0.75 mile. Look for the trail sign at the junction of the Deer Leap Mountain Trail near a boulder on your right at 0.8 mile. Keep left at this junction to remain on the Overlook Spur and continue along the rolling spruce- and fir-lined ridge until it opens onto a small, but long rock "shelf." Keeping to the left side, descend the shelf face. Just beyond the shelf, the trail opens onto the Deer Leap Cliffs Overlook at 1.0 mile. The rocks can be slippery and the overlook is quite steep, so use caution. Keep children away from the cliff's edge.

Enjoy the views of Pico Peak directly across Sherburne Pass and the sweeping views to the east and west. The remains of the old Long Trail Lodge can be seen below just south of US 4. You may also see some technical rock climbers, as this is a popular rock climbing area. After resting and enjoying the views, return to your car along the same trails, exercising caution that you go the correct way at the trail intersections.

18

Appalachian Trail: US 4 to VT 12

Total distance: 21.6 miles

Hiking time: 2 full days

Vertical rise: 5030 feet

Rating: Strenuous

Maps: USGS 7.5' Pico Peak, 7.5' Delectable Mountain, and 7.5' Woodstock North

The Appalachian Trail (AT) between US 4 at Sherburne Pass and VT 12 in Woodstock offers a very challenging 2-day backpacking trip. While the Long Trail follows the ridge of the Green Mountains, the Appalachian Trail in Vermont follows rolling terrain from the Green Mountains to the Connecticut River valley. You will hike over geological thrust faults, up and down steep slopes, across mountain meadows, along country roads, through a moss-covered gulch, and past bubbling brooks. Along the way you may meet AT through-hikers, who usually love to share stories of their long journey from Springer Mountain in Georgia on their way to Mount Katahdin in Maine.

You will also be hiking through Vermont's history, beginning at the site of the original Long Trail Lodge and ending at the site of the first ski lift in the United States. Before David Dodge invented his endless rope tow at the site in 1934, skiers had to climb up the hillside in order to ski down. Now they could be pulled up the hill by a rope tow powered by a Model T engine! The first person to use the tow, Bob Bourdon, was a friend of author Bob Lindemann. This backpacking trip is dedicated to Bob Bourdon's memory; he passed away while this edition of *50 Hikes in Vermont* was being written.

How to Get There
You begin your hike at the top of Sherburne Pass on US 4, but you must first spot a car on VT 12 in the town of Woodstock. From Woodstock (0.0), take VT 12 north past the Billings Farm and Museum (0.5 mile). At 1.6 miles pass the turn to Suicide Six Ski Area, and continue on VT 12. At 3.9 miles (0.1 mile before the Woodstock/Pomfret town line) look for a barn on the right. On the left side of the road just before the barn is a cable guard rail. The last set of cables has been removed, exposing a small drive down

to a tiny parking lot along the river. Because the lot only holds three to four cars, take as little room as possible to park.

To reach the trailhead at Sherburne Pass, take US 4 to the top of Sherburne Pass (about 9 miles east of Rutland) and the Inn at Long Trail. The inn offers parking for eight cars (no overnight parking allowed). There is also space for 25 cars on the south side of US 4.

The Trail

Day One

Total distance: 8.2 miles	
Hiking time: 5¼ hours	
Vertical rise: 2250 feet	
Rating: Strenuous	

The hike begins from the top of Sherburne Pass, former site of the Long Trail Lodge (0.0). Carefully cross US 4 and head north on the white-blazed Long Trail/Appalachian Trail. (Note that the USGS topo maps may not depict the AT's latest relocations.) You quickly ascend among some boulders until you reach a rock ledge that you drop below. Remember to watch your step through this area, especially with a full pack. Swing left past the ledge, and continue your ascent through mixed young hardwoods. You can still hear US 4 below you. At 0.5 mile you reach Maine Junction. To the left the white-blazed Long Trail continues north to Canada. You take the white-blazed Appalachian Trail, which bears to the right at this junction and continues 468 miles north and east through Vermont and New Hampshire, ending at Mount Katahdin in Maine.

Beyond the junction, the Appalachian Trail climbs gradually uphill and reaches a short spur trail to the right at 0.8 mile to an overlook called "Ben's Balcony." Take a minute to enjoy the views of Pico and Killington Peaks before a gradual descent away from the ridge. In this section you occasionally still see blue blazes along the Appalachian Trail. Do not get confused. They remain from an old practical joke when some Green Mountain Club members referred to the Appalachian Trail as a "side trail" of the white-blazed Long Trail, and thus they painted this section with blue blazes.

After your descent, enter a hardwood forest and reach Campsite #11 in Gifford Woods State Park at 1.3 miles. Turn left at the camp road and descend past the maintenance road on the right. If you need water, the park is a good place to restock your supply. Turn right onto the trail leading to VT 100 at 1.7 miles, cross VT 100, and turn right again into the Kent Pond Fish and Game Access Area.

The trail leaves the access at the right corner as you enter the lot. Going through an overgrown meadow, cross a small brook. Notice the scenic cascade on the left of the trail with views down to the pond. Pass through a mowed lawn, part of Mountain Meadows Resort, and then cross a gravel road at 2.6 miles. You then enter an area of glacial rocks and rolling terrain, ending with a very steep descent through switchbacks until you reach the end of Thundering Brook Road. Follow the road to the right until you finally reach an intersection with River Road at 4.0 miles. This road walk is rather long.

At this intersection, the Appalachian Trail goes into the woods. A sign at the road indicates you are almost at the halfway point: 4.2 miles from US 4, 5.0 miles to the shelter. Leave the road, and follow the Appa-

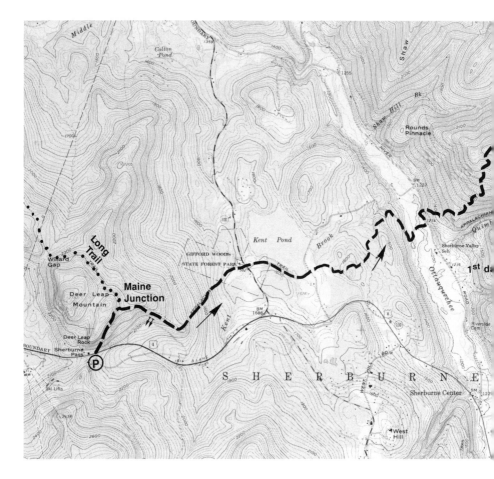

lachian Trail uphill through switch-backs to a wooded knob (no views). Then descend through deep woods to a power-line cut at 5.9 miles with views of the Ottauquechee Valley and Killington Peak. Resume your ascent through more switchbacks until another wooded knob, and then descend along a narrow ridge to yet another knob with nice white paper birch. Continue your descent along a narrow ridge, then through open hardwoods to a gulch of moss-covered rocks and conifers. This gulch is a nice change of scenery from all the rolling terrain you have just tra-versed. At 8.2 miles, a short spur to your right leads to the new Stony Brook Shelter, built in 1997 by Green Mountain Club volunteers led by Erik and Laurel Tobiasson. Water is available at the LT/AT's brook crossing just east of the shelter.

Day Two

Total distance: 13.3 miles	
Hiking time: 8 hours	
Vertical rise: 2780 feet	
Rating: Strenuous	

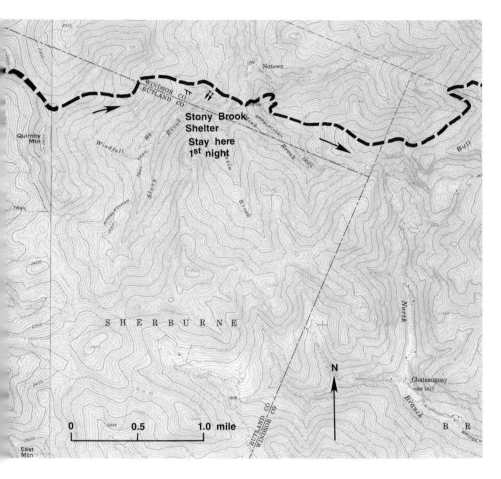

After breakfast, begin your second day by descending to a rocky overlook (0.4 miles) with a view into the Stony Brook drainage, followed by an 8-foot log ladder to help you down a steep ledge. Sit back and enjoy the view! Descend steeply to a logging road at 0.7 miles, where you turn left and then right across a bridge near an old log landing. Turn left again into the woods. After crossing Mink Brook, your route bears left and begins a steady climb via switchbacks back out of the Stony Brook drainage. At 2.6 miles you reach the height-of-land. Follow the trail down to a gully, over a few smaller hills, past several rock outcrops, and down a steep descent to the intersection of the Chateauguay Road at 4.5 miles. Beyond the road you cross old stone walls that indicate overgrown pastureland. The trail then begins a gradual climb, becomes much steeper through switchbacks, passes through a stand of white birch, and reaches a small clearing at 5.6 miles with a nice view of Lakota Lake and the White Mountains in the distance.

Descend from the clearing, steeply at first, and cross an old logging road to the bottom of a gap. Then go uphill to a relocated portion of the trail,

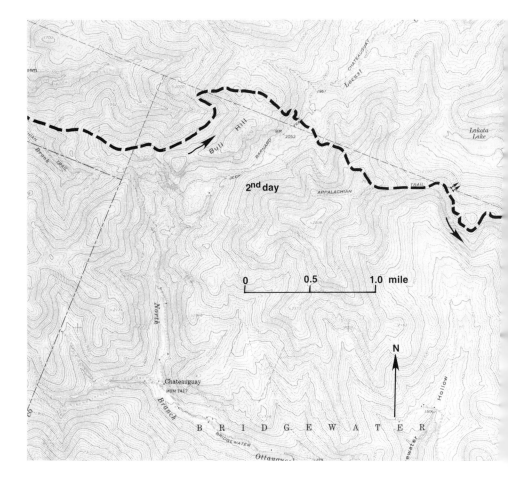

over a small knob, through a beech forest, until you reach a trail junction at 7.3 miles. To the left a spur trail goes to a private camp known as "The Lookout." Bearing right at the junction, the Appalachian Trail follows an old road that allows easy walking over gentle terrain. At 8.1 miles it reenters the woods for a short distance and then reaches and follows "King Camp Road" to the right at 8.2 miles. You soon turn left off this old road, go uphill over a ridge, and circle a small knob at 8.9 miles. You then descend again, cross a logging road, go over a small knob, and at 9.7 miles

reach the spur trail to Wintturi Shelter, where you may wish to stop and rest for a minute. Wintturi Shelter, a frame lean-to with space for six hikers, was constructed by Erik and Laurel Tobiasson and some of their friends in 1994. The shelter is named for Mauri Wintturi, an active Green Mountain Club member and trail maintainer.

From the shelter, the trail descends, follows a rocky sidehill past a huge oak tree, and crosses an old road parallel to more old stone walls for quite a distance. At the end of the stone wall to the right is a short spur at 10.7 miles to a vista of North Bridgewater. Con-

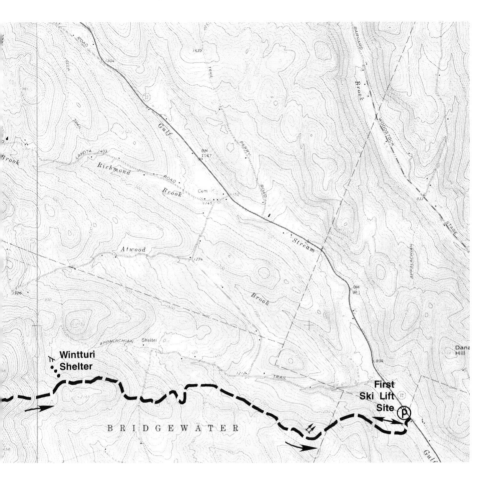

tinue downhill through a stand of sugar maples and more overgrown woods. Enter into an extensive meadow, kept open by controlled burns, until you reach a view of Mount Ascutney at 12.1 miles. Passing in and out of this meadow, you cross a snowmobile trail, swing left and reenter the woods, and at times can hear the cars on VT 12. Continue until you crest a small knoll; then descend along a narrow ridge, where you can see a deep valley to your right. At the end of the ridge, the trail opens into a large meadow with VT 12 in the valley below you. You can now see the first rope tow ski area in the United States and the small building below that housed the base of the rope tow.

Continue down through the meadow following the posts, cross the fence with a wooden stile, hike through two more pastures, and finally cross a stream on a wooden bridge to the parking lot at 13.3 miles.

19

Quechee Gorge

Total distance: 1.5 miles

Hiking time: 45 minutes

Vertical rise: 250 feet

Rating: Easy

Map: USGS 7.5' Quechee

This easy hike features spectacular views of the 155-foot-deep Quechee Gorge and the Ottauquechee River. The name Ottauquechee comes from the Natick Native American word meaning "swift mountain stream" or "cattails or rushes near a swift current."

Quechee Gorge was formed approximately 13,000 years ago, toward the end of the last glacial age. Some 6000 years prior to that, the climate warmed significantly, and the most recent glacier began to recede. A natural dam of debris (rocks, gravel, sand) formed in Connecticut, creating a narrow lake—Lake Hitchcock—up the Connecticut River valley. Similar lakes developed along the Connecticut River, including one in the Ottauquechee valley. When the dam in Connecticut broke and Lake Hitchcock drained, water

trapped in the Ottauquechee valley also broke through its dam and drained. The gushing water quickly carved through the sand and gravel to the bedrock below. The river's tremendous force and natural scouring abilities continued to carve deeply into the bedrock. From the bridge, you can see the glacial sand deposits and underlying bedrock.

How to Get There

This figure-8-shaped hike can be reached via exit 1 off I-89. If you are driving south on I-89, drive 2.5 miles west on US 4 from the exit. If you are driving north on I-89, drive 3.2 miles west on US 4 from the exit. (The exit ramps are 0.7 mile apart on US 4.) Just before the bridge on US 4 over Quechee Gorge, turn right on Dewey's Mill Road, opposite the Vermont Information Center. Continue 0.1 mile to the "Overlook Picnic & Parking" area.

The Trail

From the back of the picnic area, turn right and hike 0.2 mile to a dam, hydro-generating station, and Dewey's Mill Pond. The dam was the location of the old Dewey Woolen Mill but is now a lovely waterfall. Retrace your

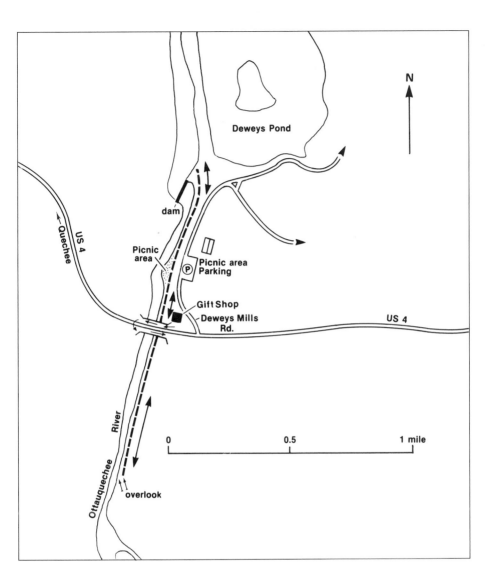

steps to the picnic area, and follow the gorge trail of crushed stone and bark behind the gift shop and under the US 4 bridge.

The gorge was once a popular resort, and the river provided power, but they were very difficult to cross. Early bridges often collapsed or were swept away by the current. The original bridge spanning the gorge was a railway bridge built in 1875 for the Woodstock Railroad. Historian William Tucker claimed that "nearly 3000 people assembled to celebrate the long anticipated event." The present steel arch was built for the railroad in 1911, but in 1933 the tracks were removed and replaced with US 4.

Continue your hike along the chain-link fence, which protects you from falling into the gorge as you descend the gorge wall to an overlook. Enjoy the views deep into the gorge. Explore the overlook area, and return to the US 4 bridge at 1.5 miles.

After going under the bridge, a trail by the gift shop leads onto the bridge, where a pedestrian walkway is provided on both sides of the road. Loop the bridge for additional views into the gorge; then return to the parking lot and picnic area.

20

Mount Independence

Total distance: 2.5 miles

Hiking time: 2 hours

Vertical rise: 200 feet

Rating: Easy to moderate

Map: USGS 15' Ticonderoga

Trillium

Mount Independence, often called the "most interesting and important historic site in Vermont," was Vermont's major Revolutionary fortification and is one of the least disturbed Revolutionary sites in the United States. The mount's chert (flintlike chalcedony rock) outcroppings and the area's abundant food resources attracted Native Americans thousands of years before European discovery. Mount Independence is protected on three sides by water and steep cliffs and is accessible only from the south. This protection, plus its 200-foot elevation above the lake, made the mount an important component of America's defense against a British attack from Canada during the war.

The northern half of Mount Independence was purchased in 1912 by Sarah Pell, who worked to preserve the site. In 1952–53 her son John, who had inherited the land, deeded the property to the Fort Ticonderoga Association, "an educational institution chartered explicitly to ensure the conservation, interpretation, and preservation of Fort Ticonderoga and neighboring sites." In 1961 and 1973 the State of Vermont purchased over 108 acres to enhance the association's effort.

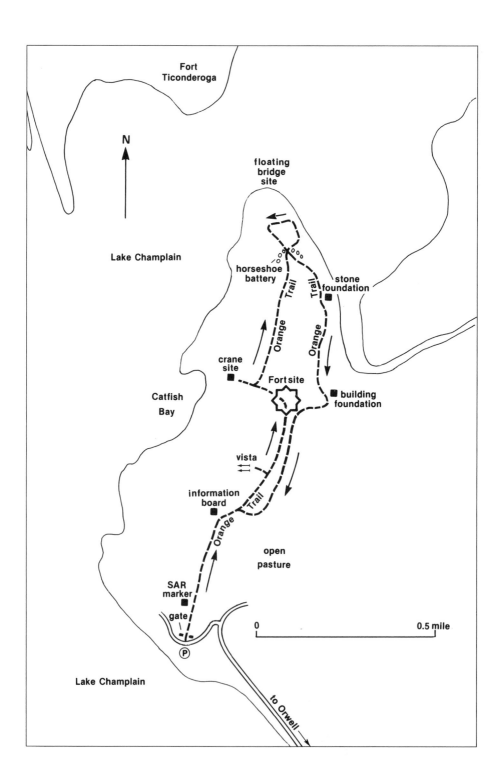

Fort
Ticonderoga

N

floating
bridge
site

Lake Champlain

horseshoe
battery

stone
foundation

Orange Trail

Orange Trail

crane
site

Fort site

Catfish
Bay

building
foundation

vista

information
board

Orange Trail

open
pasture

SAR
marker

gate

0   0.5 mile

P

Lake Champlain

to Orwell

Mount Independence is open from Memorial Day to Columbus Day, Wednesday through Sunday, 9:30–5:30. A caretaker is available to give guided tours of the site upon request. There are grazing animals on the site that should not be disturbed. Because the area is an important archaeological site held in public trust, digging, metal detecting, and artifact collecting are against the law.

The first phase in the development of a historic interpretation at Mount Independence was marked in 1989 as part of the Heritage '91 plan. Heritage '91, approved by the state legislature in 1988, is a 10-year management plan for developing and improving state-owned historic sites in celebration of the state bicentennial. After several seasons of archaeological investigation at Mount Independence, a visitors center has been built to house artifacts and provide interpretetive exhibits. The center, which opened in the summer of 1996, was designed to recede into the natural landscape, much like the historic ruins themselves.

How to Get There

To reach Mount Independence take VT 22A to the intersection of VT 73 (0.0), west of Orwell. Turn west on VT 73. At 0.3 mile bear left off VT 73 at a road junction, avoiding a side road on your left as the road swings right. At 4.8 miles the paved road turns to gravel. At 5.2 miles you reach the Catfish Bay Road junction. Turn left, and drive up the steep narrow road. At 5.3 miles park in the lot at the top of the hill on the left side of the road in a meadow.

The Trail

Begin your hike at the gate across the road from the parking lot. Bear left and go into a small wooded area, where a bronze plaque has been imbedded in a "sentry rock" by the Sons of the American Revolution. The plaque provides historical information about Mount Independence.

Return to the gate and continue to the top of the pasture, where there is an information board with trail descriptions and area maps. Although four trails lead to the mountain, this description covers the Orange Trail, which takes you 2.5 miles past several interesting historical sites.

From the information post, the Orange Trail bears north but quickly branches to the left (west) of the White Trail. You soon pass over the top of the mountain and reach an overlook of Lake Champlain and Mount Defiance. Continue between woods and pasture on easy grades to a clearing, where you bear left at 0.5 mile. Logs have been placed on the ground to indicate the layout of the Star Fort, the central stronghold on Mount Independence. The square parade ground is marked by cedars that have grown up along the lines of the barrack walls. Just ahead is an old well believed to have originated in the Revolutionary War period.

At 0.6 mile you reach a spur trail to the site of a huge crane used to hoist cannons, equipment, and supplies up to the fort from ships anchored below in Catfish Bay. Continue your hike through the woods to a clearing, at 0.8 mile, that was the site of shops for blacksmiths, armorers, rope makers, wheelwrights, and other skilled craftsmen. Return to the woods, where you soon see a monument in the middle of a horseshoe-shaped battery. Here, cannons once commanded Lake Champlain to the north and the narrows between Mount Independence and Fort Ticonderoga. Next, descend to a shore battery that once guarded the vulnerable north shore of Lake Champlain. Continue your descent to the shoreline and the former site of a floating bridge that connected Mount Independence and Fort Ticonderoga. The bridge was 12 feet wide and anchored to 22 sunken piers. The trail follows the shoreline to an outcrop above the lake where ships are believed to have been masted.

Next, leave the shoreline, return to the horseshoe-shaped battery, and bear left to complete your loop. As you pass through a wooded area at 1.7 miles, look for the foundation of a possible observation shelter and another old rectangular foundation. At 2.0 miles you again cross logs that indicate the outline of the fort. Hike through the pasture, and return to the information board at 2.5 miles.

The Orange Trail is typical of the other three trails on Mount Independence. If you have time, consider exploring the other sites.

21

Mount Horrid Overlook

Total distance: 1.4 miles

Hiking time: 1 hour

Vertical rise: 620 feet

Rating: Moderate

Map: USGS 7.5' Mount Carmel

This short steep hike takes you to the top of the "Great Cliff." According to a Green Mountain National Forest sign:

The rock that makes up the exposed face of this cliff was formed during earliest geological times. Freezing and thawing have wedged off fragments which have accumulated over time on the mountain slope.

Be aware that the trail may be closed when peregrine falcons are nesting on the cliff overlook. Before they were reintroduced by the state into the area, falcons had not nested on these cliffs for 50 years. A nesting pair released several years ago has returned to the area. Peregrine falcons are extremely sensitive to human disturbance, especially from above, and may abandon their nest if approached too closely. Please obey all posted trail signs during nesting season, and see the introduction for more information on the falcons.

How to Get There

Take VT 73 to the top of Brandon Gap. Just west of the gap summit, there is a parking lot for 30 cars on the south side of the road. Before parking your car, however, stop at the pull-off area just east of the gap summit for a view of the cliffs and a beaver pond as well as information boards describing the cliffs and pond ecology. After enjoying the views, return to the parking lot at the top of the gap.

The Trail

Cross VT 73, climb the bank, and begin hiking north on the white-blazed Long Trail. You cross a small raspberry patch and ascend to a Green Mountain National Forest registration box and sign that indicates a distance of 0.6 mile to the "Great Cliff" overlook.

After the sign, the trail steeply ascends on log steps to a ridge at 0.2 mile. Birches line the trail along the ridge until you ascend more steps. The trail swings to the western side

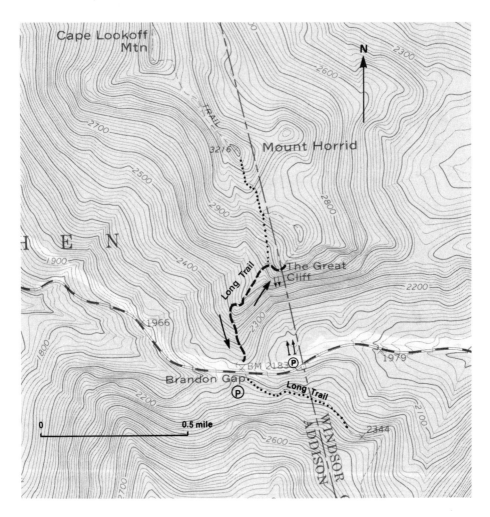

of the ridge, passes through mixed hardwoods, and becomes much rockier and steeper. When climbing steeply over rock steps that may be slippery if conditions are wet, watch your step and stay on the trail to limit erosion in this area. After hiking among some rocks, notice a birch stand just ahead and, at 0.6 mile, a blue-blazed trail on your right that leads uphill through the birches to the "Great Cliff" at 0.7 mile. As you step out into the opening, you are on top of the 2800-foot Mount Horrid Overlook seen from the parking area—now 700 feet below you. Also below you is the beaver pond you saw from the pull off.

After enjoying the views, including Bloodroot Gap to the south, hike back down the same trail to Brandon Gap. The descent is easier, but watch your footing, especially on steep sections in wet conditions.

22

Rattlesnake Point

Total distance: 3.9 miles

Hiking time: 3 hours

Vertical rise: 1160 feet

Rating: Moderate

Map: USGS 7.5' East Middlebury

Rattlesnake Point, a large rock outcrop at the southern end of Mount Moosalamoo, provides spectacular views of two lakes and the regions beyond. This trail, which begins on Green Mountain National Forest land, was completed in 1977 by the Youth Conservation Corps and rebuilt in 1983 by a crew from the Rutland Community Correctional Center. This blue-blazed United States Forest Service (USFS) trail begins a loop that links the Falls of Lana Picnic Area, Rattlesnake Point, Mount Moosalamoo, and the Moosalamoo Campground.

How to Get There
The trail is located on VT 53, 6 miles north of VT 73 in Forest Dale or 3.5 miles south of US 7 near Middlebury. A USFS sign marks the correct park-ing area 0.2 mile south of the Branbury State Park entrance on the east side of the road. Be sure to avoid the first USFS "Falls of Lana" parking area 0.1 mile south of the park!

The Trail
Although somewhat obscure, the trail climbs the small bank behind the parking area and quickly reaches the gated USFS access road to Silver Lake. Turn right, and follow the road on easy grades. You soon reach a sign-post that indicates you are entering the Green Mountain National Forest Silver Lake Recreation Area, advising that motorized vehicles are prohib-ited to "Preserve the quiet so seldom found in today's world." It also indi-cates a distance of 0.5 mile to the Falls of Lana, and 1.5 miles to Silver Lake.

Ascend the road along switchbacks until you enter a clearing where a power line and penstock descend from Silver Lake to a power station on VT 53 below. (A penstock is a pipe that carries water.) Through the clearing are views down to Lake Dunmore. Beyond the power-line cut, the road begins a gradual ascent and soon reaches a wooden sign on your left as you start to hear Sucker Brook and

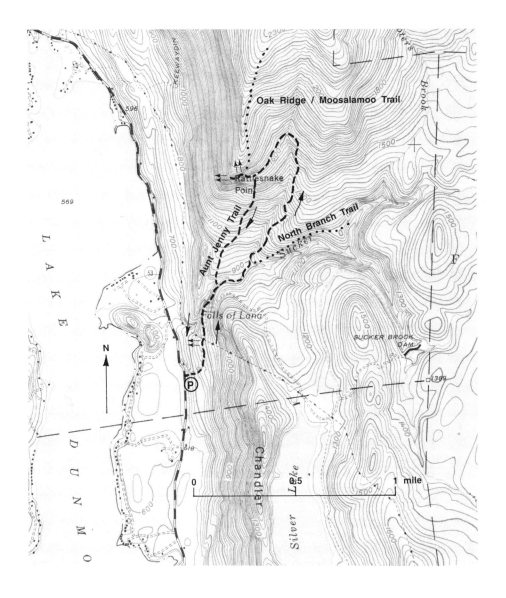

the Falls of Lana. Take a minute to enjoy the view of the falls, which you can see from behind the sign. The Falls of Lana were discovered in 1850 and named by a party of soldiers for their commander, General Wool who, during a tour of duty in Mexico, was known as General Lana, the Spanish word for wool.

Continue your hike along the road parallel to Sucker Brook until you reach the Silver Lake Trail junction and some outhouses at 0.5 mile. Hike parallel to the brook until you cross it on a wooden bridge about 100 yards from the trail junction. Just beyond the wooden bridge you reach another blue-blazed trail junction, which leads straight ahead to the Rattlesnake Cliffs Trail. A sign indicates it is 1.8 miles to the cliffs from this junction.

Hike along Sucker Brook on the blue-blazed Rattlesnake Cliffs Trail. You soon reach a registration box at the junction with the Aunt Jenny Trail, which will be your return route. Continue on the Rattlesnake Cliffs Trail past this junction along the old road and brook to a grassy clearing at 0.8 mile. The signpost at the clearing indicates the junction with the North Branch Trail on your right.

Follow the Rattlesnake Cliffs Trail left at this junction. Note the marker indicating that the Youth Conservation Corps constructed this trail in 1977. After crossing a small brook, follow the trail steeply past several large boulders, through a level area, until you ascend again along switchbacks toward a small valley. Climb steeply out of the valley until you reach the upper end of the Aunt Jenny Trail at 1.75 miles. Note this intersection because the Aunt Jenny Trail will be your return route.

Beyond the junction you again climb a steep sidehill on a series of steps designed to help control erosion. Take time to enjoy the occasional views you get along this section of trail. At 2.0 miles the Oak Ridge Trail to Mount Moosalamoo enters on your right. Bear left at this junction, and continue along the trail, enjoying views of the lake below. You reach the junction of the West Cliff Overlook Trail at 2.1 miles. Take this trail for a view down to Lake Dunmore; then return to the junction. Continue on the Rattlesnake Cliffs Trail to the South Lookout, which descends to an open rock overlook of Silver Lake and Lake Dunmore at 2.3 miles. In addition to the gorgeous view, Rattlesnake Cliffs also offer a treasure of blueberries in season, so keep an eye out for them, as well.

After enjoying the view, reverse your route along the same trail to the junction of the Aunt Jenny Trail at 2.8 miles. In the early 1900s hikers used to enjoy stopping at Aunt Jenny's Tea Room, a favorite resting spot and refreshment stand. The tearoom, located just south of the Silver Lake Power Station, was operated by Mrs. Jenny Dutton Rickert.

Continue your hike by turning right and descending along the Aunt Jenny Trail, which is a bit steeper but passes through a beautiful oak forest. At the trail junction at 3.4 miles, turn right to return to the picnic area, the Falls of Lana Overlook, and the Silver Lake Trail back to the parking area at 3.9 miles.

23

Robert Frost Trail

Total distance: 1-mile loop

Hiking time: 1 hour

Vertical rise: 120 feet

Rating: Easy

Map: GMNF 7.5' East Middlebury

Robert Frost spent 23 summers in a small cabin in the Ripton area. This trail, constructed in 1976 by the Youth Conservation Corps, commemorates his poetry. Several of Frost's poems are mounted on plaques along the loop trail, and various signs describe the natural environment. You may also wish to stop at the Robert Frost Wayside Recreation Area, with picnic tables and information boards, 0.2 mile east of the trailhead on VT 125.

How to Get There

The trail is located 2.1 miles east of Ripton, or 9.8 miles from Hancock, on the south side of VT 125. There is a United States Forest Service (USFS) trailhead parking area for 10 to 20 cars. An outhouse is provided. A trail map signboard at the parking area shows the location of the trail system. A handicapped-accessible trail loop is included at the beginning of the trail system.

The Trail

From the signboard, bear left and follow the gravel path past a sign that lists significant dates and facts about Robert Frost. You soon reach a junction, where you bear left and cross the south branch of the Middlebury River on a bridge. After the bridge, turn right and ascend to a softwood grove overlooking the river. Here, the trail swings left and follows easy grades through the forest. Signs along the way identify many of the trees and plants.

At 0.5 mile you enter an open meadow and reach a bench. A sign provides profiles of the area mountains, including Firetower Hill, Bread Loaf Mountain, Battell Mountain, Kirby Mountain, and Burnt Hill. The trail swings left through the meadow and comes to a bench overlooking the river. Prescribed burning is used to keep the meadow open and en-

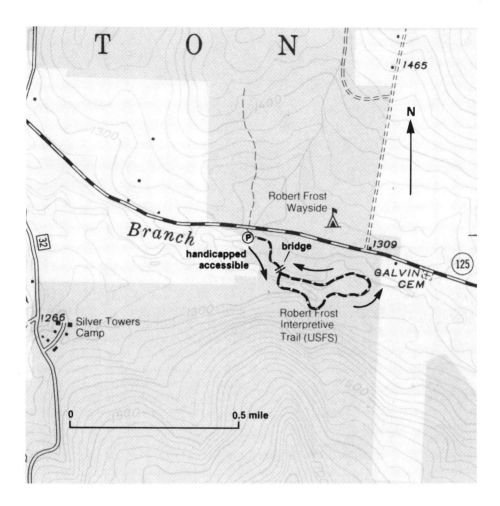

courage the growth of blueberries and huckleberries.

The trail parallels the river, enters the woods, and returns to the bridge. At the Y, bear left to cross a large wooden bridge over a swamp. Then turn right and hike back to the parking area.

24

Texas Falls

Total distance: 1.2-mile loop

Hiking time: 1 hour

Vertical rise: 160 feet

Rating: Easy

Map: USGS 7.5' Bread Loaf

Impressive waterfalls and geological formations make this interpretive trail an enjoyable, easy hike through part of the Green Mountain National Forest. Texas Brook, part of a watershed that drains this 9-square-mile area, begins approximately 3 miles to the north as a seasonal stream, then makes its way to Hancock Branch, the White River, the Connecticut River, and, finally, the Atlantic Ocean.

How to Get There

Drive west on VT 125 from the VT 100/VT 125 intersection in Hancock (0.0) to the signpost for "GMNF Texas Falls Recreation Area" at 3.0 miles. Go north on the access road to a small parking area on your left at 3.5 miles. (Additional parking is available at a picnic area up the road at 3.75 miles.)

The Trail

The trail begins opposite the parking area, where you see and hear Texas Falls. Elaborate stone steps and walls descend to the falls and provide breathtaking views into the deep ravine.

Cross the bridge over Texas Brook, turn left, and ascend upstream on more steps. You soon reach a registration box, which provides interpretive pamphlets for two interconnecting nature trails. The first trail follows the stream for 0.3 mile, then takes the road back to the parking area. The second trail continues along an upper trail 0.75 mile in a loop back to the falls. Benches along the way allow you to linger, read the guide, and enjoy the trail.

As you walk upstream, still in sight of the brook and road, note the exposed roots and rocks along the trail. This erosion is caused by people walking off the trail and compacting the ground so that the roots are unable to penetrate the hard soil. Please help stop further erosion by staying on the trail.

As you continue your hike through the evergreen forest, be sure to enjoy the fragrant air. The pamphlet explains that evergreens are "ever green" because their leaves are more efficient

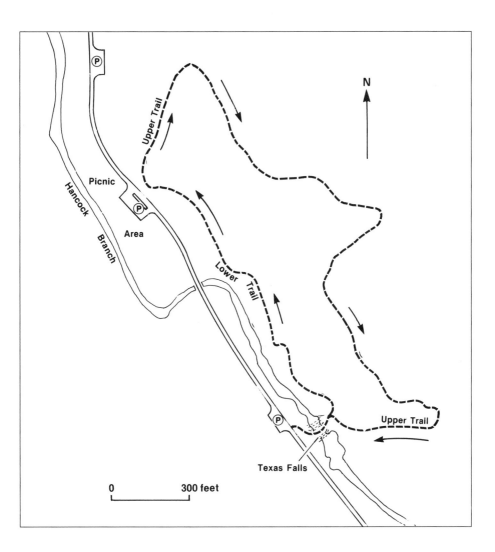

than those of deciduous trees at re-taining life-sustaining water during the winter. Adaptations include a smaller surface area, a waxy coating, and an antifreezelike resin.

As you gently climb along the wide, gravel trail, be sure to look for old aspen trees and lichens that appear on boulders. Also, take time to rest on one of several benches. The trail continues along a fern-covered bank to the crest of a hill. Hike down the hill, look for a bridge, and read the plywood disk designed to help you identify area trees. At 0.3 mile drop off your pamphlet at the registration box and descend to the road and your car, or continue along the upper trail.

To continue your hike, turn right and climb along an old logging road that is also used for winter snow-mobiling. The trail soon takes a sharp right and climbs to the top of the next rise as you pass through a stand of mixed hard- and softwood trees. At 0.6 mile, you cross two small brooks and then descend to a hemlock stand. Continue downhill to the falls and over a bridge. After a few steps and switchbacks, follow the loop trail down into the gorge. A side trail to your left descends to a lookout. At 1.1 miles, return the pamphlet to the registration box, recross the brook, marvel again at the beautiful falls, and continue to the picnic area for lunch.

25

Skylight Pond

Total distance: 4.6 miles

Hiking time: 4–5 hours

Vertical rise: 1620 feet

Rating: Moderately strenuous

Map: USGS 7.5' Bread Loaf

Skylight Pond is a high-elevation pond located on the Long Trail between Battell and Bread Loaf Mountains. Moose have occasionally been sighted at this shallow pond, and the sundew, a carnivorous bog plant, lives along the pond's shore.

How to Get There

From the center of Ripton (0.0), drive 2.8 miles east, or 9.0 miles west of VT 100 on VT 125, to United States Forest Service (USFS) Road–FR 59. Follow FR 59 north to Steam Mill Clearing on the right side of the road at 3.6 miles. Parking for 10 to 15 cars is provided at the clearing.

The Trail

The blue-blazed trail enters the woods along an old logging road parallel to a brook. You soon reach a registration box, where you should sign in both for safety reasons and to provide trail-use data to help trail maintenance and protection programs.

The trail bears right at a fork, and crosses the brook on puncheon. You then enter an area of former logging activity, now overgrown with yellow birch, beech, and maple trees. Numerous old logging roads intersect the trail, so be careful to follow the blazes. Crisscross the brook and start to ascend at 0.4 mile. Deep water bars help stop trail erosion, as well as discourage vehicles from using the old roadway. You soon reach a signpost indicating that you are entering the Bread Loaf Wilderness. Established in 1984, the 21,480-acre Wilderness includes 17 miles of the Long Trail, 11 major peaks (all over 3000 feet in elevation), and the Presidential Range (Mount Wilson, Mount Roosevelt, Mount Cleveland, and Mount Grant).

As the trail ascends, you cross the brook twice. There are limited views of the Bread Loaf Mountain ridgeline along this section of the trail. Continue through a wet area on an old overgrown road, cross the brook, bear right, and follow along the brook.

Skyline Lodge at Skylight Pond

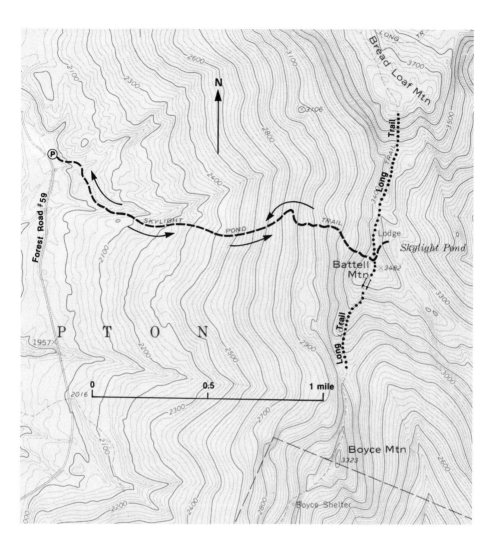

Cross the brook again and swing right, go back onto the road, and then take a sharp right off the road. At 0.7 mile you cross a wet area as the trail winds uphill along a series of switchbacks.

At 1.1 miles you have limited views of Bread Loaf Mountain to the north. Follow a brook gully toward a notch in the ridgeline through a forest of yellow birch, spruce, and hemlock. You soon start a steeper climb around a small spruce and balsam knob. You can see the summit ahead after cresting the knob at 1.6 miles. The ridge opens up into a sunny path, but you soon return to the denser softwoods and ascend again.

Enjoy the views to the west as you begin a steep climb through several large boulders to the actual ridgeline. Continue uphill to the Long Trail junction, where the sign indicates a distance of 2 miles back to your car. The shelter is on the side trail straight ahead, but first turn right and follow the Long Trail to an unmarked side trail on your right. This spur trail leads to a great western overlook, at 2.1 miles, of Lake Champlain and the Adirondack Mountains. Return to the junction, and take the side trail down to Skyline Lodge and Skylight Pond at 2.4 miles.

A new cedar log shelter, Skyline Lodge, was built in 1987 by the United States Forest Service and the Green Mountain Club to replace the old shelter, which had deteriorated and become unsafe. Several thousand pounds of 20-foot cedar logs, cement, and other materials were airlifted to the site by the Vermont Air National Guard. Now one of the nicest shelters on the Long Trail, the lodge looks out over beautiful Skylight Pond.

After resting at the shelter, return to the junction at 2.6 miles, and hike back down the trail to your car.

26

Bread Loaf Mountain

Total distance: 8.6 miles

Hiking time: 5 hours

Vertical rise: 2235 feet

Rating: Strenuous

Map: USGS 7.5' Lincoln and 7.5' Breadloaf

Bread Loaf Mountain, so called because its long ridgeline profile resembles a loaf of bread, marks the halfway point along the 270-mile Long Trail. An overlook near the wooded summit offers beautiful views to the west.

How to Get There

Take the Lincoln-Warren Highway, 1.0 mile east of Lincoln, or 3.7 miles west of the Lincoln Gap summit, to the road crossing of the New Haven River. Turn south on United States Forest Service (USFS) Road–FR 57 (0.0), and drive 4.2 miles through South Lincoln and along the river to the junction of FR 201. Drive to and park at a "USFS Dispersed Camping Site" at 4.6 miles.

The Trail

At the trailhead note the Cooley Glen Trail (see Hike 28), which continues along the gravel road. Instead take the Emily Proctor Trail on your right, which begins with a steep climb along an old road. At the top of the hill at 0.2 mile you begin to notice an extensive burned area on your right. The trail bears left around the burn, a log road enters on your right, and you soon reach a hiker registration box. The trail then follows a wide woods road and enters the Bread Loaf Wilderness at 0.5 mile. Continue along the trail on easy grades with occasional views of the ridge on your left across the valley. This is a good section to stretch your legs for the climb ahead, which is quite rocky—so watch your footing.

At 1.0 mile you cross a brook that is a branch of the New Haven River. You soon cross it a second and a third time. For the second crossing, note the high-water route on your right. At 2.0 miles the trail forks. Follow the left fork and begin to ascend. Look for views of Bread Loaf Mountain on your right. As the ascent gets steeper, you cross several small brooks, and at 3.2 miles the character of the woods changes from birches

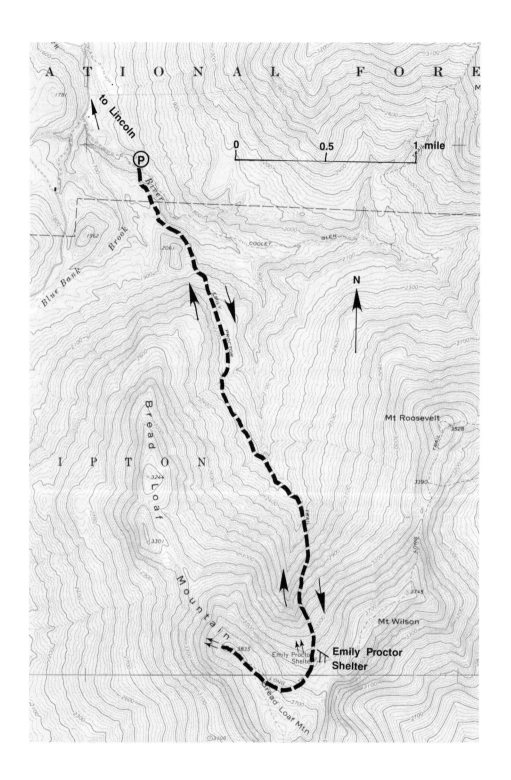

to Lincoln

0   0.5   1 mile

N

Mt Roosevelt

Emily Proctor
Shelter

First Long Trail patrol truck

to spruce and fir. During the steep ascent, occasional level spots offer you a chance to rest and enjoy views of the valley below.

At 3.5 miles you reach the Emily Proctor Shelter and a well-deserved rest. From the shelter there are excellent views of Mount Grant and Mount Abraham to the north. Named for an avid hiker and supporter of the Green Mountain Club during the early 1900s, the shelter is a log structure built in 1960 by the Long Trail Patrol; the roof and foundation were replaced in 1963 by the Youth Conservation Corps. The Long Trail Patrol was founded in 1929 when the Green Mountain Club decided it needed a summer patrol to help with trail maintenance. The patrol, which still exists today, helps to maintain and blaze the trail, and report on trail conditions.

Beyond the shelter, follow the white-blazed Long Trail to your right (south) along a gentle uphill. You will find this section of trail much easier than your climb up to the shelter. Extensive trail work, including rock water bars and ditches to control erosion, has been done along the trail up the ridgeline of Bread Loaf Mountain. At 4.2 miles the trail appears to double back on itself as you reach the halfway point of the 270-mile Long Trail, a point very symbolic to end-to-end hikers. Take the signed and blue-blazed Overlook Trail that leads to your right to the 3835-foot summit and an overlook at 4.3 miles.

This western overlook provides beautiful views of Lake Champlain and the Adirondacks beyond. The yellow buildings below are the Bread Loaf Campus of Middlebury College. You also see the Snowbowl Ski Area to the south, as well as Killington Mountain in the distance.

After you have rested and enjoyed the views, hike back down the same trails to your car.

Trail up Snake Mountain

27

Snake Mountain

Total distance: 3.5 miles

Hiking time: 2½ hours

Vertical rise: 980 feet

Rating: Moderate

Map: USGS 7.5' x 15' Port Henry

Hiking Snake Mountain is an adventure. Not only will you find a beautiful summit view, you will also enjoy oak forests, rare plants, old foundations and roads, and an area rich in Vermont folklore and history. While enjoying the views from the summit, consider that 14,000 years ago you would have been standing on an island in Lake Vermont! Lake Vermont covered this region from the Adirondacks to the Green Mountains except for a serpentine ridge—from which Snake Mountain derives its name.

Please respect other trail users you may encounter along your journey. Because the trail and summit of Snake Mountain are part of the 999-acre Snake Mountain Wildlife Management Area, hikers, skiers, mountain bikers, and hunters all use these multi-purpose trails.

How to Get There

Go to the junction of VT 17 and VT 22A (0.0) in Addison. Drive south on VT 22A for 2.9 miles to a left turn onto Willmarth Road. Continue on Willmarth Road to the junction of the Mountain Road at 3.5 miles. The trail begins at the end of Willmarth Road. Park along the shoulder of Mountain Road. Please respect the landowner by not parking near the house.

The Trail

The blue-blazed trail up Snake Mountain begins beyond the orange gate. Follow easy grades through an old overgrown pasture, where you will easily see the succession of growth from former uses of this land. At 0.6 mile the road reaches a junction. To your right is the former trail. Take note of this junction so you do not miss the turn on your return trip down the mountain. Turn left onto the blazed carriage road, being careful to avoid a faint trail that enters on your left. Occasional red blazes are property lines. In season this is an ideal area for beautiful spring flowers.

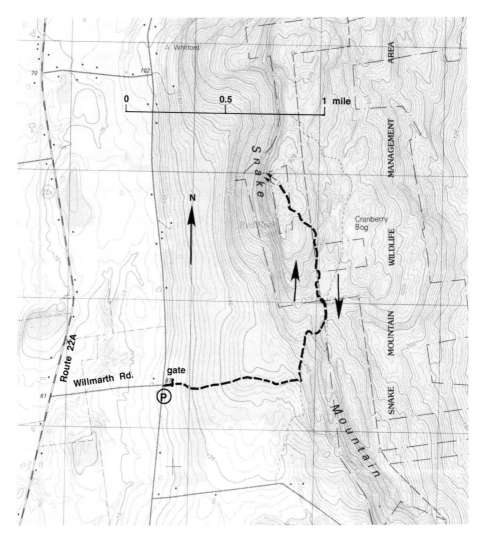

Continue your hike along the road, which begins to get steep and has deep water bars to control erosion. At 1.0 mile the road swings right, then left onto a switchback along the steep bank. Avoid the old road on the right in the middle of the switchback. Please stay on the main road—the switchbacks are used to control erosion.

After the switchbacks the grade moderates, and another old overgrown road enters on your right at 1.1 miles.

Cross a small valley and continue through an oak forest, where you will probably see an abundance of happy, noisy squirrels. Old roads continue to intersect the main route, so be sure to stay on the main road, which gets rockier and then levels off at 1.6 miles. As you near the summit, numerous old roads continue to intersect the main carriage trail. At 1.7 miles the road swings to the west and enters a clearing at 1.75 miles.

The abundance of roads on Snake

Mountain originated in the 1800s, when the mountain was the site first of a sawmill and then the Grand View House, which opened on the summit in 1874. The Grand View House was a popular destination for summer outings. In fact, for a time the name of the mountain was changed to "Grand View Mountain" because the founder of the summit house, Jonas Smith, thought the name Snake Mountain would discourage people from visiting his hotel. Mr. Smith also built two towers on the summit, first a wooden one and then a replacement one of steel; he charged his guests a fee to climb and see the view.

Life on the mountain changed a great deal in the early 1920s and '30s. The Grand View House was permanently closed in 1925, the road to the summit was washed away in the flood of 1927, the hurricane of 1938 destroyed the tower, and fire eventually burned down the house. The old foundation is well hidden but still visible if you explore the summit.

The concrete pad on the summit overlook is not, as many suspect, the foundation of the old hotel but rather the foundation of a house a young man attempted to build on the summit before he died overseas in a car crash. The State of Vermont eventually acquired the summit land in 1988.

From the concrete pad you can enjoy 180-degree views of Addison County and Lake Champlain, plus a view of Dead Creek below. Dead Creek, a spidery body of water surrounded by rich farmland, is part of the Dead Creek Wildlife Management Area and a favorite spot for canoers, duck hunters, and birders. The area maintains restricted and important waterfowl nesting areas.

If you choose to explore the summit area looking for old foundations and building remains, be sure not to get lost. After resting, enjoying the views, and possibly exploring, return to your car via the same route.

28

Mount Grant

Total distance: 8.4 miles

Hiking time: 5 hours

Vertical rise: 1960 feet

Rating: Strenuous

Map: USGS 7.5' Lincoln

The scenic Cooley Glen trail up Mount Grant follows old logging roads along the New Haven River. Though overgrown in places, the logging roads are dry and follow gradual grades, except for very steep sections near the top of the trail. Several swimming holes in the river provide the opportunity for a refreshing summer splash after (or maybe even before) your long hike.

How to Get There
Take the Lincoln-Warren Highway, 1.0 mile east of Lincoln, or 3.7 miles west of the Lincoln Gap summit, to the road crossing of the New Haven River. Turn south on United States Forest Service (USFS) Road–FR 57 (0.0), and drive 4.2 miles through South Lincoln and along the river to the junction of FR 201. Drive to and park at a "USFS Dispersed Camping Site" at 4.6 miles.

The Trail
At the trailhead register, note the Emily Proctor Trail, which turns right. Instead, take the blue-blazed Cooley Glen Trail that follows the gravel road along the New Haven River. Cross the river on a bridge at 0.3 mile and reach a clearing, once an old log landing. The trail leaves the far end of the clearing at a deep ditch and follows the river on almost level grades over a wide, overgrown old logging road. You soon see a road junction as the trail bears right and parallels the river. At 1.0 mile you cross several deep water bars and tributaries as you move away from, and then return to, the river. No blazes are visible along this portion of the trail, except for occasional blue-blazed rocks in the grassy road.

At 1.5 miles the road becomes quite wet and rocky. Enter the woods to avoid this wet area, and then return to cross a tributary near the remains of an old bridge. This point marks the entrance to the Bread Loaf Wilderness, which was named for 3835-foot Bread Loaf Mountain. Established in 1984, the 21,480-acre Wilderness

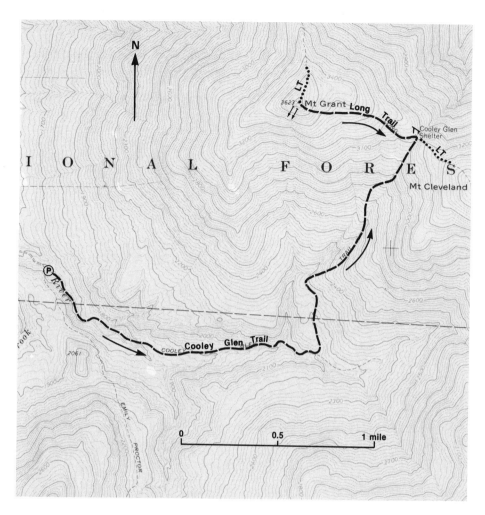

includes 17 miles of the Long Trail, 11 major peaks (all over 3000 feet in elevation), and the Presidential Range (Mount Wilson, Mount Roosevelt, Mount Cleveland, and Mount Grant).

Continue your hike—moving away from the river—ascend slightly, and swing left along the old road. Blue blazes can be seen on the trees. At 1.9 miles you climb until you pass through a scenic, more mature forest. At 2.5 miles the trail levels after a short ascent, and you can see Mount Grant through the trees on your left. The trail ascends steeply along a gully, passes through a rocky nettle patch, then crosses the small brook you could hear during your climb up the gully. Begin a long hike uphill, cross a small brook, pass a spur trail, and reach the junction of the Long Trail at 3.3 miles.

Turn left and follow the white-blazed Long Trail north several yards to Cooley Glen Shelter. The shelter, built by the United States Forest Service in 1965, is a frame lean-to with bunk space for six to eight hikers. Take time for a well-deserved rest.

Beyond the shelter, continue north on the Long Trail. The hike to Mount Grant's summit is easy compared to the trail you just climbed. Look for southern views before the trail swings right and you ascend again. By 4.0 miles the mixed forest turns to predominantly spruce. The trees become more stunted as you hike along switchbacks to the southern overlook. Just beyond is the 3623-foot wooded summit of Mount Grant at 4.2 miles. From the southern overlook you can see the New Haven River basin, Mount Cleveland, Mount Roosevelt, Mount Wilson, and Bread Loaf Mountain.

Hike back down the same trails to the parking area at the campsite.

29

Lincoln Gap

Total distance: 1.25 miles

Hiking time: 1 hour

Vertical rise: 600 feet

Rating: Easy to moderate

Map: USGS 7.5' Lincoln

Even though this is a short hike, it is quite scenic, especially during fall foliage season, with excellent western views of the Green Mountain range. The trail passes through the Bread Loaf Wilderness, named after Bread Loaf Mountain, the highest point in the wilderness. Established in 1984, the 21,480-acre wilderness includes 17 miles of the Long Trail, 11 major peaks (all over 3000 feet in elevation), and the Presidential Range (Mount Wilson, Mount Roosevelt, Mount Cleveland, and Mount Grant).

How to Get There

To reach the trail from the eastern side of the mountain, take VT 100 to Lincoln Gap Road (the sign says "Lincoln Gap/Bristol") (0.0) near Warren. Turn west off VT 100 onto Lincoln Gap Road. The road turns to dirt at 1.6 miles. At 2.8 miles the road is paved and ascends to the top of the gap at 4.3 miles.

From the western side of the mountain, drive east from Bristol (0.0) on VT 116/VT 17 to the turnoff to Lincoln and Lincoln Gap at 1.6 miles. Take this turnoff to the town of Lincoln at 5.1 miles. You reach a bridge and United States Forest Service Road 54 at 6.2 miles. At 7.5 miles the road turns to dirt. At 9.3 miles the road turns to pavement again and reaches the top of the gap at 9.9 miles.

Parking for eight cars is available just to the east of the gap summit. An additional parking lot holding 15 to 20 cars is located to the east of the upper lot.

The Trail

From the upper parking area, take the white-blazed Long Trail south from the gap. As you enter the woods, climb a small bank until you reach a Green Mountain National Forest registration box. A sign tells you that you are entering the Bread Loaf Wilderness. To the left is a steep ridge you will be climbing—but first begin a moderate ascent through yellow and white birches un-

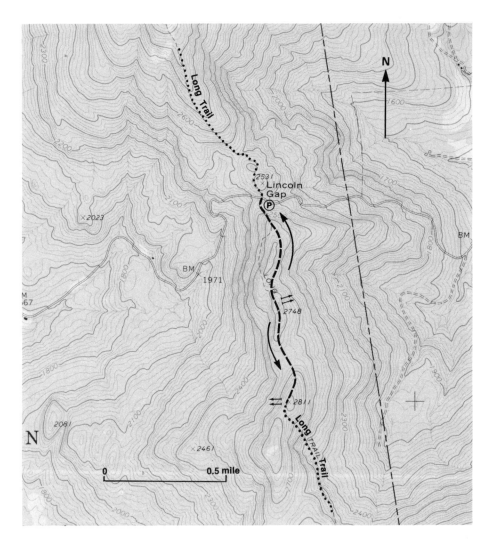

til you reach a double blaze and the first switchback. Turn left and begin a steep ascent. Partway up the ridge, rest and enjoy the view into the gap below. Notice metal signs on the trees, which indicate the location of a benchmark— a surveyor's mark made on a permanent landmark of known position and altitude, used as a reference point in determining other elevations.

Continue your ascent with limited views into the gap and of Mount Ab-

raham to the north. Be sure to avoid all side trails in this section. Swing around the east ridge on a more gradual slope, and begin a steep scramble over quite rocky terrain. The trail then follows along the ridge, opening up to good views east to Warren and the valley below and north to Mount Abraham. Continue your hike into the woods, across a wet area, and up another rocky section of trail. Notice the steeper slopes on both

Lincoln Gap overlook

the west and east sides of the trail as you ascend along a densely wooded ridge.

As the trail begins to descend slightly through softwoods, you step out onto Eastwoods Rise, an exposed rock face at 0.6 mile. Enjoy the excellent views: west to Bristol and the Bristol Cliffs, south to Mount Grant, and north to Mount Abraham.

Hike back down the same way to your car, but be extremely careful as you descend the rocky sections of the trail.

30

Mount Abraham

Total distance: 5.2 miles

Hiking time: 5 hours

Vertical rise: 2500 feet

Rating: Strenuous

Map: USGS 7.5' Lincoln

The spectacular views from the 4006-foot summit of Mount Abraham make this hike one of the most popular in Vermont. On a clear day you can see the Adirondack Mountains in New York, the White Mountains in New Hampshire, and the Green Mountain range from Killington Peak to Belvidere Mountain.

How to Get There
Start in the town of Lincoln. At a rock memorial marker in the center of town (0.0), take a left (north) on Quaker Street. Pass the Town Clerk's office on your right. At 0.7 mile turn right (east) on United States Forest Service (USFS) Road–FR 350, and proceed up a long hill. At 2.0 miles you reach a fork where you bear right, still on FR 350. The road becomes much narrower. Stay left on FR 350 at another fork. Continue to the parking area on your left, which has room for six cars, at 3.2 miles.

The Trail
Begin your hike across from the parking area at the trailhead sign, which indicates a distance of 2 miles to the Long Trail and the Battell Shelter. Enter the woods on the blue-blazed Battell Trail, and quickly reach a trail register. Swing left and ascend a moss-covered hill. The trail then levels and you enter a sugar bush, where sap is collected from the sugar maple trees.

Over the years, Vermont sugar makers have produced more maple syrup per year than any other maple-syrup-producing state: depending on spring weather, up to 500,000 gallons each year. Approximately 40 gallons of maple sap, collected in the sugar lines you pass, produce just 1 gallon of pure maple syrup. Vermont maple syrup is required to have a heavier density than US standards and to be free of preservatives. Look for "Vermont Maple Syrup" on the labels if you decide to take some home with you.

After you pass under and along

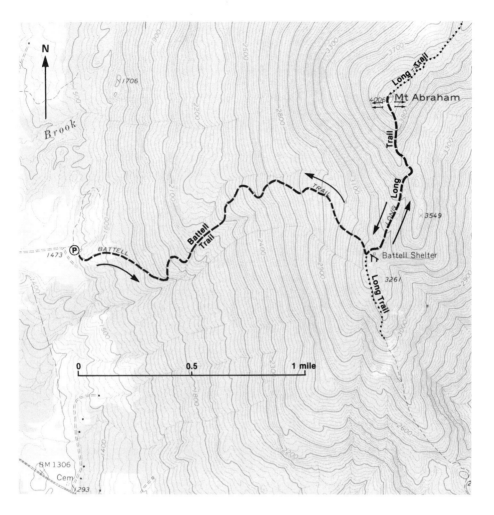

several sugar lines, cross a wet area on flat rocks and ascend some steep switchbacks. Portions of the upper sugar lines can be seen off the trail. At 0.7 mile the trail bears right and ascends to a brook crossing. The trail soon becomes rocky and turns left on an old road at 1.2 mile. (Note this junction for your return hike.) The wide road continues uphill on a steep grade over long switchbacks and enters some softwoods. The road, less defined because of erosion, may be wet in places. Cross a small brook at 1.8 miles, and then leave the road for only a short distance. Ascend the rocky, eroded road to the Long Trail junction at 2.0 miles.

Hike straight uphill on the Long Trail to the Battell Shelter. The trail in this section, quite wide and on easy grades, follows an old carriage road built in the late 1800s by Joseph Battell, proprietor of the Bread Loaf Inn. The Battell Shelter, constructed in 1967 by campers from Farm and Wilderness Camps using materials airlifted to the site by helicopter, has bunk space for six to eight hikers and is maintained by the Green Mountain Club and the United States Forest Service. A small spring is located 100 feet east of the shelter.

Continue uphill on the Long Trail along the very rocky old carriage road, with occasional views of the summit ahead. At 2.3 miles leave the roadway and hike up steep grades, often on exposed bedrock scars. Look south and enjoy views back to the trail you just climbed. Next, scramble up an exposed rock face, and return briefly to smaller softwoods before you begin your final ascent to the summit.

The trees are now waist high as you ascend to the open rock summit at 2.9 miles. Three small rock walls provide shelter from the winds as you enjoy one of the best panoramic views in Vermont. To the east are the White Mountains of New Hampshire; to the west are the Bristol Cliffs, Lake Champlain, and New York's Adirondack Mountains; and to the south and north are the Green Mountains—from Killington Peak to Belvidere Mountain.

The summit supports a community of small, rare, arctic-alpine plants—the patches of "grass" and soil among the summit rocks. While on the summit, avoid disturbing any of these endangered plants by hiking only on the trail and rocks. For more information on this unique ecosystem, see the introduction.

Hike back down on the same trails to your car.

31

Monroe Skyline

Total distance: 11.1 miles

Hiking time: 1½ days, 1 night

Vertical rise: 2520 feet

Rating: Moderate

Maps: USGS 7.5' Mount Ellen and 7.5' Lincoln

The Long Trail between Lincoln Gap and the Appalachian Gap (VT 17) is one of the most scenic ridge walks in Vermont. You pass over six mountain summits, three of which are over 4000 feet in elevation. The Long Trail from Lincoln Gap to the Winooski River is called the Monroe Skyline, after Professor Will S. Monroe, who was instrumental in relocating the trail along this ridgeline.

Your first day is very short (1.8 miles), so you have time to spot cars and arrange equipment. You can also become familiar with carrying a pack if this is a new or infrequent experience. You can begin on Friday afternoon, as long as you leave ample time (about 2.5 hours if you haven't hiked in a while) to reach the Battell Shel-

ter before dark. Also, since the first day is a short hike, you might consider carrying some extra food/weight for your evening meal.

The second day start early, with a climb up Mount Abraham. Spend the day hiking along the ridgeline, where you enjoy some spectacular views of Vermont, New York's Adirondack Mountains, and New Hampshire's White Mountains. In addition, the ridge is popular with glider pilots, who may sail overhead during your hike. You finish your journey at the Appalachian Gap on VT 17.

How to Get There

Spot a car at the Long Trail parking area on VT 17 at the height-of-land called the Appalachian Gap, which is 6.3 miles west of Irasville and VT 100; 9.6 miles east of the VT 17 and VT 116 intersection; and 12.9 miles east of Bristol.

Your hike will begin at the small parking area just east of the height-of-land in Lincoln Gap. To reach the gap from the eastern side of the mountain, take VT 100 to Lincoln Gap Road (where the sign says "Lincoln Gap/Bristol") near the town of Warren (0.0), where you turn west. The road

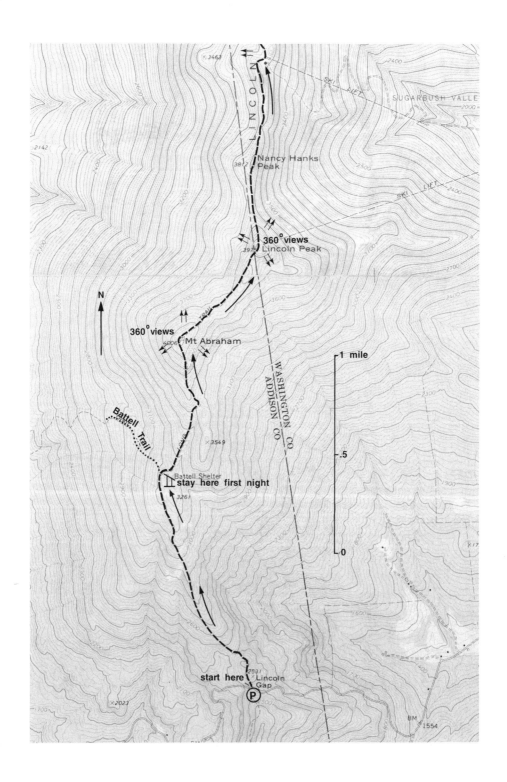

LINCOLN

2142

Nancy Hanks
Peak

3812

360° views
Lincoln Peak

N

360° views

×3006 Mt Abraham

1 mile

WASHINGTON CO
ADDISON CO

.5

Battell Trail

×3549

Battell Shelter
stay here first night

3261

0

K 17

start here
Lincoln
Gap

P

×2023

2531

BM
1554

SKI LIFT

SUGARBUSH VALLE

SKI LIFT

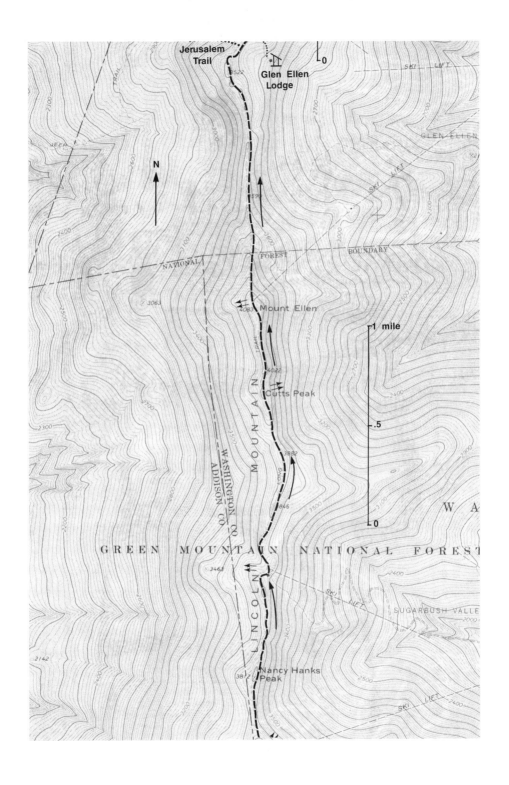

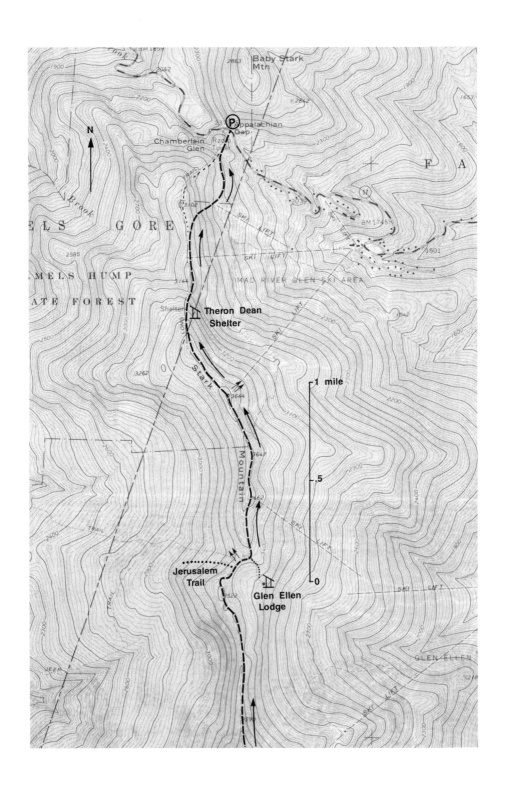

turns to dirt at 1.6 miles. At 2.8 miles the road turns back to pavement and ascends to the top of the gap at 4.3 miles.

From the western side of the mountain, drive east of Bristol (0.0) on VT 116/VT 17 to the turnoff to Lincoln and Lincoln Gap at 1.6 miles. Take this turnoff to the town of Lincoln at 5.1 miles. You reach a bridge and United States Forest Service Road 54 at 6.2 miles. At 7.5 miles the road turns to dirt. At 9.3 miles the road turns to pavement again and reaches the top of the gap at 9.9 miles.

The Trail

Day One

Total distance: 1.8 miles

Hiking time: 2 hours

Vertical rise: 825 feet

Take the white-blazed Long Trail north from the gap to a Green Mountain National Forest registration box and sign in. Then hike up the hillside parallel to the roadway below you. Swing right, climb a small knob, and descend on log steps into a col (a saddlelike depression in the crest of a ridge), where the trail switches back along a rock shelf. At 0.4 mile you begin your ascent up the northwestern ridge of Mount Abraham. The trail is quite steep in places as you ascend a series of plateaus through mixed hard and softwoods.

At 0.8 mile red blazes mark a property line. Climb up an exposed rock ledge scar until you reach a short spur to the left and a good view to the west. Descend into a deep softwood stand, and then hike up along a mixed hardwood ridge. A clearing covered with ferns provides a brief break, especially

on a sunny day. Pass between two large boulders called "the Carpenters," after two trail workers, and enter another dense softwood stand with a view of Mount Abraham. Now on easier grades, you cross a brook and reach the Battell Trail junction at 1.7 miles.

The trail in this section, quite wide and on easy grades, follows an old carriage road built in the late 1800s by Joseph Battell, proprietor of the Bread Loaf Inn west of Middlebury Gap. In 1901, he cut a trail north to Mount Ellen, possibly the first skyline trail in the Green Mountains.

Turn right at the junction, and ascend the Long Trail to the Battell Shelter, which has bunk space for six to eight hikers, where you spend the night. The Battell Shelter was constructed in 1967 by campers from Farm and Wilderness Camps using materials airlifted to the site by helicopter and is maintained by the United States Forest Service and the Green Mountain Club. A small spring is located 100 feet east of the shelter.

Day Two

Total distance: 9.3 miles

Hiking time: 8 hours

Vertical rise: 1695 feet

If you start very early in the morning, you can climb Mount Abraham in time to see the sun rise over the White Mountains to the east and the valley below covered in a carpet of mist. Just be careful because the steep, rocky trail is difficult to hike at dawn.

Begin your day's hike uphill on the Long Trail along the old carriage road, with occasional views of the summit ahead. At 0.2 mile you leave the roadway and hike up steep grades, often on exposed bedrock. Look south and enjoy

The view toward Bristol and the Adirondacks from the Monroe Skyline

views back down the trail. Next, scramble up an exposed rock face, return briefly to smaller softwoods, and begin your final climb to the summit. The trees are waist high as you ascend to the open rock summit at 0.8 mile. Three small rock walls provide shelter from the winds as you enjoy one of the best panoramic views in Vermont. To the east, New Hampshire's White Mountains; to the west, the Bristol Cliffs, Lake Champlain, and New York's Adirondack Mountains; to the south, as far as Killington Peak; and, to the north, as far as Belvidere Mountain. The summit supports a small, rare arctic-alpine plant community, so walk only on the rocks to avoid disturbing any of these endangered plants or the surrounding soils. See the introduction for more information. Beyond the summit, enter the woods and continue along the ridge until you reach the summit of Little Abe and the 3975-foot summit of Lincoln Peak at 1.6 miles.

As you enter the ski clearing, make a sharp left down to the woods on the west side of the summit. Be very careful of your footing on the exposed rocky west slope, especially since the dramatic views of the Bristol area cause your attention to wander. You return to the woods and follow the now wide and fairly level trail to a lookout of Sugarbush. Allow time to enjoy the view and take a rest.

Continue your hike over the rocky trail on easy grades until you ascend Nancy Hanks Peak (named after a member of a prominent local family) at 2.2 miles and descend to the Castlerock Chair Lift. Bear left and follow the ski trail to Holt Hollow at 3.0 miles, where the trail enters the woods. A spring is located 200 feet west of the trail.

Ascend the ridgeline over rolling terrain to the 3022-foot summit of Cutts Peak at 4.1 miles, where a rock outlook provides another place to rest and enjoy the beautiful view. After descending Cutts Peak, climb to the wooded 4083-foot summit of Mount Ellen, the third-highest mountain in Vermont. Just past the summit is the upper station of the Glen Ellen Chair Lift and good views north of General Stark Mountain, Camel's Hump, and Mount Mansfield. Past the station, the trail makes a sharp left and returns to the woods to avoid the ski trails. Descend the steep western face of the mountain until you reach the northern boundary of the Green Mountain National Forest at 4.9 miles.

Here the character of the trail changes abruptly; the forest is denser, there are fewer views, and the ridge is covered with large, moss-covered boulders. At 6.3 miles you reach the Jerusalem Trail junction. Stay on the Long Trail, and ascend a small knob to Orvis Lookout. Continue to the Barton Trail junction, which leads about a quarter mile to Glen Ellen Lodge, which was built in 1933 by the Green Mountain Club's Long Trail Patrol. There are excellent eastern views from the lodge of the Mad River Valley, Northfield Mountains, Granite Mountains, and White Mountains in New Hampshire.

Return to the junction, and begin your last major ascent up the west ridge of General Stark Mountain. After reaching the summit, the Long Trail continues along the ridge and follows a ski trail to the top of Mad River Glen's Chair Lift and Stark's Nest at 7.3 miles. Hike uphill past the building, then bear left into the woods. You briefly enter the ski trail before returning to the woods. Scale down over the ridge's exposed rock face, occasionally grabbing rocks and lowering yourself over the rock. A ladder is even provided in one particularly difficult spot. After your descent, bear left and follow the moss-covered rock face to the Theron Dean Shelter at 8.0 miles. (Theron Dean was an active member of the Green Mountain Club during the Club's early years and a close friend of Will Monroe.) After resting at the shelter, take a short spur trail on the left to Dean Panorama, your last wide panoramic northern view. Continue down to Dean Cave, a short underground passage that leads back to the main trail 150 feet from the upper junction. Hike along the main trail until you approach a chairlift. Just before the lift, bear left, hike through the woods, and ascend a small rock face. Follow the trail on moderate grades over long switchbacks through a scenic birch forest. Climb over one final knob before descending to VT 17 and the end of your hike at the Appalachian Gap at 9.3 miles.

NORTHERN VERMONT

32

Spruce Mountain

Total distance: 4.5 miles

Hiking time: 3 hours

Vertical rise: 1340 feet

Rating: Moderate

Map: USGS 7.5' East Barre

This trail leads to an abandoned fire tower as well as several lookouts with excellent views of northern and central Vermont and western New Hampshire. Children especially enjoy exploring a very large split rock 1.6 miles along the trail.

Most of the trail up Spruce Mountain is located in the L.R. Jones State Forest, a 642-acre parcel of land located in Plainfield. This forest, the first parcel purchased by the state of Vermont, on November 24, 1909, was formerly called the Plainfield State Forest. The name was changed to honor Professor L.R. Jones, a University of Vermont professor of botany, for his efforts to establish the State Tree Nursery and create the position of State Forester. The summit of Spruce Mountain is located in Groton State Forest.

How to Get There

Take US 2 to Plainfield. Turn south at the flashing yellow light (0.0), cross a bridge, and bear left. At 0.4 mile turn right on East Hill Road, which quickly turns to gravel. At 2.0 miles Spruce Mountain is visible ahead. At 3.6 miles cross a small bridge and go straight. As you go downhill at 4.3 miles, turn left. At 4.7 miles bear left at a bend in the now twisty and bumpy road. At 5.4 miles turn right, and drive past the site of the old gate and parking area to a new parking area for 10 to 15 cars and a second gate. Please park in this upper lot, which is located on state rather than private land.

The Trail

Begin your hike along the roadway past the gate. During this 1-mile road walk, notice the frequent views of Spruce Mountain, the fragrant spruce-scented air, and, in the fall, a few beautiful full-color maple trees along the way. Also, look for ruffed grouse in the woods—you may startle one into sudden flight. Although numerous old logging roads intersect the roadway, be sure to stay on the main road. Don't be concerned that you appear to be walking away from Spruce Mountain.

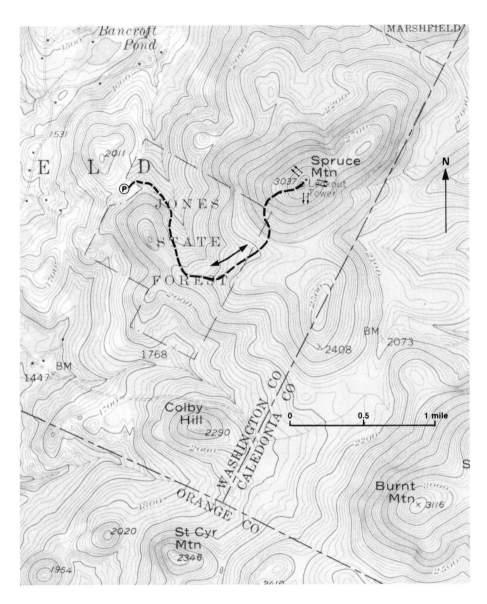

At 1.0 mile, a wooden sign indicates that the trail and road bear left. You soon cross an unusual area of small, round rocks—or as one hiker describes it, "a baby boulder field"— where the road ends. The relatively level, rocky trail continues past a large boulder engulfed by the roots of a birch tree. You soon cross a brook on puncheon, and at 1.5 miles you turn right and climb a switchback to avoid an old eroded part of the trail. The ascent is quite steep. The trail finally levels somewhat, and you reach a large rock outcrop split by the freezing and thawing of water. This is a good place

to take a break and explore the rock.

The trail continues past the rock and ascends along a hillside by the bottom edge of a sloping, exposed rock slab. Follow the slab to 1.9 miles, where you swing right for a steeper ascent. The trail returns to a mix of hard- and softwoods and enters a small open area of ferns before returning to the woods. Bear right into a rocky area on your left, and continue until you reach an overlook on your right.

Immediately to the left of the overlook is the summit, with an old fire tower and the remains of a ranger's cabin. The original tower was built in 1919 and used until 1931, when it was replaced and the cabin was built. In 1943 the current steel lookout tower was transferred to Spruce Mountain from Bellevue Hill near St. Albans. Though not used as a fire tower since around 1974, it was repaired and repainted in 1987.

A rock outcrop on the summit provides a nice view of Groton State Forest, including Pigeon and Noyes Ponds. From the tower, enjoy extensive views of central Vermont, the Green Mountain range, and western New Hampshire.

After enjoying the views, hike back down the same trail to your car.

33

Owl's Head/ Groton State Forest

Total distance: 0.5 mile

Hiking time: 30 minutes

Vertical Rise: 160 feet

Rating: Easy

Map: USGS 15' Plainfield

This relatively short hike takes you to the summit of Owl's Head in Groton State Forest. The summit's stone fire tower, the trail, and the picnic shelter at the trailhead were constructed in the 1930s by the Civilian Conservation Corps (CCC).

The second largest contiguous landholding by the state of Vermont, Groton State Forest is a scenic wilderness and one of the most popular recreational areas in northern Vermont. It has been used since the early 1890s for hunting, swimming, boating, hiking, fishing, berry picking, skiing, and, more recently, snowmobiling. Because the land was too rocky to farm, area residents used the region's forests of spruce, hemlock, beech, birch, maple, and white pine for fuel and lumber and to make potash for fertilizer and soap.

Since acquiring the first tract of land in 1919, the state of Vermont now owns approximately 25,000 acres in Groton State Forest. It is managed by the Vermont Department of Forests, Parks and Recreation for summer and winter recreation, forestry, and as wildlife habitat.

Exposed mountain peaks in the forest display a granite bedrock similar to that of New Hampshire's White Mountains. This forested wilderness supports a variety of wildlife, such as black bear, moose, deer, mink, beaver, otter, fisher, grouse, loons, herons, and many other bird and mammal species.

How to Get There

Drive north on US 2 from Marshfield Village (0.0) to the junction of VT 232 at 1.0 mile. Turn east on VT 232 and drive past the New Discovery Campground entrance at 5.3 miles. Continue beyond this entrance to a left turn marked by an "Owl's Head" sign at 6.6 miles. Turn left and follow this steep gravel road to the parking lot and picnic pavilion at 7.6 miles.

The Trail

From the parking lot, turn right and walk to the picnic pavilion, where a signboard describes summer activities

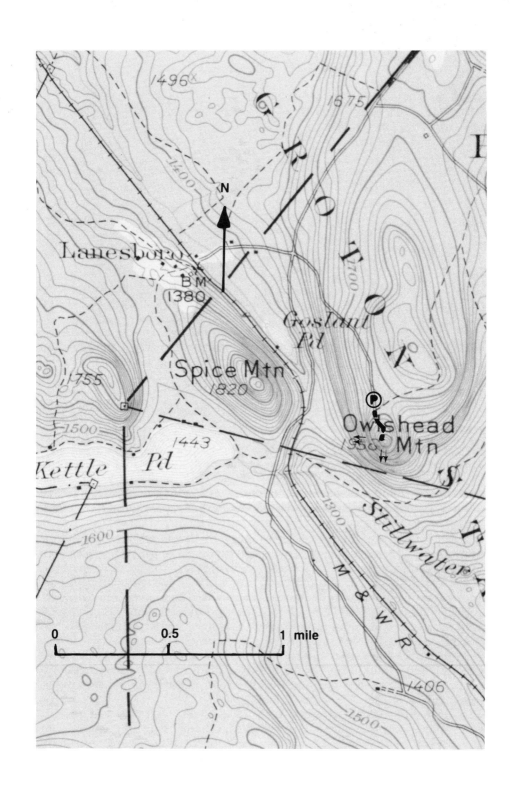

N

1496×

1675

G
R
O
T
O
1700

Lanesboro

BM
1380

1400

Gostant
Pd

1755

Spice Mtn
1820

1500

1443

Kettle   Pd

Owlshead
1950 Mtn

P

Stillwater

1600

1500

M & W R

S

0   0.5   1 mile

1406

1500

Fire tower on Owl's Head summit

and programs as well as hiking opportunities in the park. Take a moment to enjoy the view of Kettle Pond from the picnic pavilion overlook.

Your walk begins behind the picnic shelter and heads toward the outhouses visible from the parking lot. Turn right on the main trail and begin a very gradual hike through mixed hardwoods up the first set of CCC-constructed steps. You soon reach another set of steps as the trail bears left and begins a series of short switchbacks. Be sure to avoid all unblazed side trails and take time to notice the extensive CCC rock work.

At 0.25 mile you reach the top of Owl's Head and the octagonal stone fire tower. A rock outcrop beyond the tower provides fantastic views of Groton State Park. Visible to your right is Kettle Pond, and to your left is Osmore Pond surrounded by Big Deer and Little Deer Mountains. To the southeast are approximately 850 contiguous acres of mature, first-growth paper birch, red maple, and aspen, the result of intense fires around the turn of the century. This area is logged during the summer to disturb the soil enough to create an ideal seed bed for the favored species of paper and yellow birch. Directly south is a 200-acre northern hardwood stand being regenerated to encourage aspen reproduction. Buds of mature male aspen trees are a highly preferred winter food source for ruffed grouse.

Take a short spur that leads north to another view of Osmore Pond. Hike back down the same trail to your car.

34

Mount Philo

Total distance: 0.2 mile (plus optional 1 mile summit road walk)

Hiking time: 1 hour

Vertical Rise: 50 feet

Rating: Easy

Map: USGS 7.5' Mount Philo

This very short, easy trail, located in the 160-acre Mount Philo State Park, provides an excellent view of New York's Adirondack Mountains, a nice opportunity for a picnic lunch, and the option of a 1-mile road walk around the summit area.

How to Get There
Drive 1.2 miles north on US 7 from North Ferrisburg or 2.5 miles south on US 7 from the stoplight on US 7 near Charlotte. Turn east at the blinking yellow light (0.0) to Mount Philo State Park. You reach the park gate at 0.5 mile. A day-use fee is charged.

Drive through the gate and ascend Mount Philo by car. The road soon forks and becomes one way. Notice remnants of old roads and paths, con-

crete steps, an old spring, culverts, and a gravel pit. The summit cliff is on your left as you drive to the southwestern side of the mountain for the final pitch to the top of the toll road. At the summit is a parking lot for 50 to 60 cars.

The Trail
Your minihike starts at the summit parking lot. You will note a contact station and a large picnic area. The station and fire tower were established in the mid-1920s. Between 1938 and 1940 the Civilian Conservation Corps (CCC) constructed a steel tower, which was abandoned by the 1960s and finally removed in the early 1970s.

From the western end of the lot, descend past a picnic pavilion to a large rock face with guard rails. As you stand on the summit of Mount Philo and overlook what is now the Champlain Valley, contemplate that Mount Philo was once an island in the Champlain Sea. According to a booklet published by the state of Vermont, two different areas of rock were thrust over each other approximately 4.7 billion years ago: This low-angle thrusting was succeeded by high-angle faulting. The park rocks were subjected

View from Mount Philo

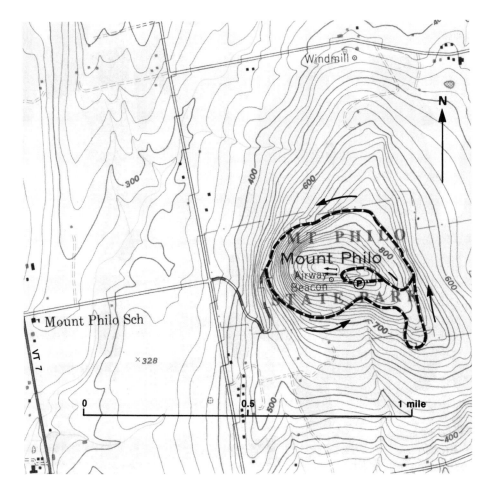

to weathering and erosion for over 300 million years, or until glaciers advanced over the area less than 60,000 to 70,000 years ago. Advancing glaciers scoured the rock; retreating or wasting glacial ice left deposits of clay, sand, and gravel in the park. A series of lakes formed south of the northward wasting glacial ice and deposits of beach gravel and lake sand formed along the slopes of Mount Philo, which was then an island. An arm of the sea next advanced southward into the Champlain Valley, leaving marine beach gravels just west of Mount Philo. The marine waters eventually retreated, and present-day Lake Champlain came into existence.

Just north of the rock overlook, a trail descends to an even better vista. Return to the first overlook, and, if you choose, hike the summit road loop, which provides additional views to the west and south.

35

Hires and Sensory Trails/Green Mountain Audubon Nature Center

Total distance: 1.25-mile loop (total for the two hikes described)

Vertical rise: 200 feet

Rating: Easy

Maps: USGS 7.5' Hinesburg and 7.5' Huntington

Both of these easy trails are located in the Green Mountain Audubon Center, a 230-acre nature center owned and operated by the Green Mountain Audubon Society, a local chapter of the National Audubon Society. The grounds are open every day from dawn to dusk. The visitors center is open weekdays and weekend afternoons, depending on staff availability, and offers a Summer Ecology Day Camp, seasonal programs, workshops, classes, and more. We recommend that you pick up its brochure and map of the trails at the visitors center. Donations to maintain the center are welcome,

and you can also purchase a variety of books and other items.

The Hires Trail goes to a lookout with an unusual view of both Mount Mansfield and Camel's Hump. The Sensory Trail, with a rope leading through fields and woods, is designed as both a hiking trail for the blind and visually impaired and as a way for others to enjoy and experience the area through their other senses. Please remember to stay on the trails, and do not remove any natural objects from the area.

How to Get There

To reach the Green Mountain Audubon Center, take exit 11 off I-89 (0.0) and turn left (east) onto US 2. Drive 1.6 miles to Richmond, and, at the traffic light, turn right (south) on Bridge Street toward Huntington. At 1.9 miles you cross the Winooski River. The road bears right and winds uphill before leveling again. Stay on the main road as it bears left at two junctions. At 6.7 miles you reach a sign and turn right to find the center. Parking for 8 to 10 cars is located at the visitors center, where a trail signboard shows the location of the numerous hiking trails.

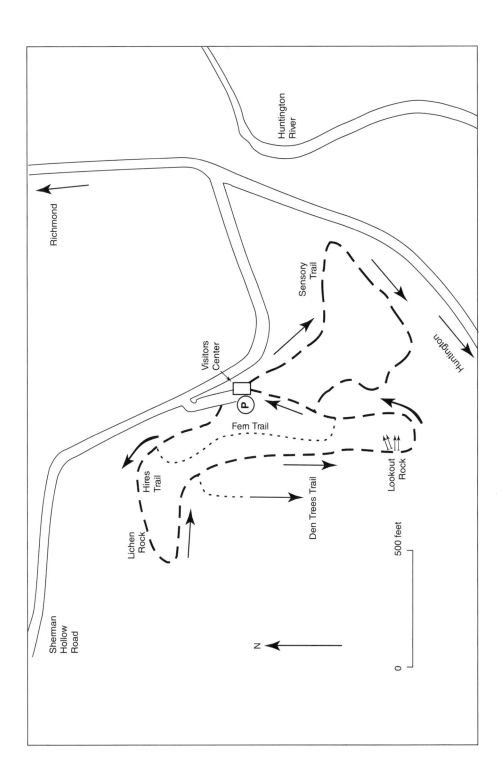

Huntington River

Richmond

Sensory Trail

Visitors Center

Huntington

P

Fern Trail

Hires Trail

Lichen Rock

Den Trees Trail

Lookout Rock

Sherman Hollow Road

N

500 feet

0

Hires Trail: This trail was named for Christine L. Hires, who donated the land for the center. The trail starts to the right, behind the signboard. Hike up a short bank, bear right at an obscure junction, and climb some old wooden steps through young mixed hardwoods. You quickly reach a junction with the Fern Trail on your left. Stay on the Hires Trail. Notice that you are hiking parallel to Sherman Hollow Road as you walk up the hillside on moderate grades. You soon bear left and climb through birches and then small softwoods. A bench provides an excuse to take a rest and enjoy the tranquility and wildlife.

Continue uphill to a spur trail on your right that leads to Lichen Rock, a large moss-covered boulder. Return to the main trail and quickly reach a junction. Follow the unblazed main trail uphill along several rock outcrops until you pass through mixed hardwoods and reach a rock shelf called Lookout Rock at 0.4 mile. Enjoy the nice views of Camel's Hump and an unusual view of Mount Mansfield to your left. From the overlook, gradually descend through young mostly maple hardwoods until you are below the overlook. You soon intersect the other end of the Fern Trail and begin a moderate descent to a junction with the Sensory Trail on your right. Leave the woods, enter an overgrown field, cross a mowed lawn, and reach the visitors center at 0.7 mile.

Sensory Trail: This very unique trail begins on the porch of the visitors center, crosses fields, winds through the woods, and, at 0.5 mile, loops back. What makes the trail unique is its design for the blind and visually impaired. A rope, strung between posts, provides a guide for the trail. For those who are not blind or visually impaired, close your eyes and notice the difference without the security and benefit of sight. You begin to rely more strongly on your other senses and more fully appreciate the sounds and smells around you. Any description would be woefully inadequate—this trail must be experienced to be enjoyed!

36

Camel's Hump

Total distance: 7.4-mile loop

Hiking time: 6 hours

Vertical rise: 2645 feet

Rating: Strenuous

Maps: USGS 7.5' Waterbury and 7.5' Huntington

This difficult hike takes you to the 4083-foot summit of Camel's Hump. The Waubanaukee Indians called Camel's Hump *Tah-wak-be-dee-ee-wadso*, which means "the saddle mountain." Legend says that Samuel de Champlain's explorers thought the mountain looked like a resting lion and so called it *le lion couchant,* or "the couching lion." In 1798, Ira Allen referred to the mountain as Camel's Rump on a historical map. From that name, Zadock Thompson in 1830 called the mountain Camel's Hump.

During the Civil War, Camel's Hump was a well-known resort with horse and carriage trails leading to guest houses at the base and summit. Its popularity waned, however, with competition from the Mount Mansfield

resort complex. In the early 1900s, area businessmen restored the trails and the summit house. Professor Will Monroe of the "Couching Lion Farm" (the trailhead of this hike) continued their efforts by developing a section of the Long Trail known as the "Monroe Skyline."

In 1911, Colonel Joseph Battell gave 1000 acres of land, including Camel's Hump, to the state of Vermont for one dollar, specifying that the entire forest be "preserved in a primeval state." Through various purchases, exchanges, and gifts, the state acquired approximately 7478 acres by 1951.

The Department of Forests, Parks and Recreation defended a policy of limited building and regulated development on the Hump until the summit and surrounding state land were declared a Natural Area in 1965. In 1968, the Hump was designated a Registered National Natural Landmark by the National Park Service. The Camel's Hump State Forest, established by the Vermont legislature in 1969, includes all lands extending from VT 17 north to the Winooski River and from the Huntington River to the Mad River. The park now includes 19,474 acres of land.

Camel's Hump in winter

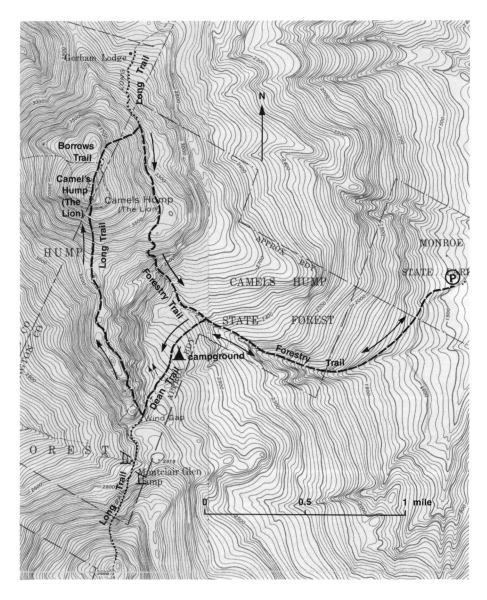

Camel's Hump is one of the highest use areas in Vermont. Mostly visited by day hikers, the mountain averages 10,000 to 15,000 hikers a year. Take time to observe the width of the trails and the extensive trail work required by the heavy foot traffic. Such heavy use requires extensive and difficult trail maintenance and constant attention to the protection of the summit's fragile arctic-alpine vegetation, much of which looks like ordinary grass. Excessive trampling of plants and soil leads to loss of rare vegetation, so it is very important to stay on marked trails and rock outcrops. Green Mountain Club/state ranger-naturalists, on duty during the hiking season, assist hikers and explain the fragile nature of this environment. Be sure to follow their instructions. For additional information on this unique plant community, see "Arctic-Alpine Vegetation" in the introduction.

How to Get There

Begin at the junction of US 2 and VT 100 just off exit 10, I-89 (0.0) miles in Waterbury. Drive south toward the town of Waterbury. At 0.1 miles, turn right onto Winooski Street and then cross the Winooski Street bridge. After crossing the bridge, turn right onto the River Road at 0.4 miles. Continue on River Road and at 5.0 miles, turn left (south) onto Camel's Hump Road. There are several side roads off the Hump Road, so be careful to stay on the main road. At 6.4 miles bear left at the fork and cross the bridge. At 8.7 miles, parking for 20 to 25 cars is available at the Couching Lion Farm parking lot at the end of the road. Parking is also available in an additional lot located at the foot of the hill before you drive up to Couching Lion Farm.

The Trail

Follow the blue-blazed trail from the parking area into the woods, and come to a trail registration box and information board. Because you will be following several trails throughout this loop hike, take time to review the information board and trail map before beginning your hike. From the registration box you follow the blue-blazed Monroe and Dean Trails.

After crossing a brook, pass by old stone walls and an overgrown pasture. Cross another brook at 0.8 mile, and climb to a trail junction at 1.3 miles.

To your right is the Monroe Trail on which you will return. Turn left along the Dean Trail. At 1.5 miles you cross Camel's Hump Brook and soon pass the Hump Brook Tenting Area. Continue uphill, cross a birch-covered knob at 2.0 miles, and reach an area with a view over the beaver pond to Camel's Hump.

Beyond the pond, the Dean Trail ascends through a notch to the Long Trail junction. The trail ahead leads 0.2 mile to Montclair Glen Lodge, a frame cabin with bunks for 12, built in 1948 by the Long Trail Patrol. During the hiking season a Green Mountain Club caretaker is in residence, and a small fee is charged for overnight use. A sharp left turn takes you to the Long Trail south via the Allis Trail.

Turn right (north) on the white-blazed Long Trail, and steeply ascend past the rock face you saw from the beaver pond. At the top of the rock face there is a nice view of the pond and valley below and Mount Ethan Allen to the south. The trail climbs along the rock outcrop, enters a cleft in the rock at 2.6 miles, and reaches an overlook. Ascend another knob, and enjoy the view ahead of the rocky Camel's Hump summit.

Next, descend toward the west side of the ridge, drop into a col with occasional views, and ascend again at 3.4 miles. There are several views of the summit as you steeply traverse the southwest face of the mountain. At 3.8 miles you reach the Alpine Trail junction. This yellow-blazed trail can be used to bypass the summit in bad weather. Continue north on the Long Trail, hike up the exposed western face of the Hump, and reach the 4083-foot summit at 4.0 miles. Remember the fragile nature of this summit area, and be sure to stay on the marked trails and rock outcrops. Help to protect this endangered ecosystem.

On a clear day there are spectacular views from the summit. To the south are Mounts Ethan and Ira Allen, Lincoln Ridge with wide ski trails, and Killington and Pico Peaks. To the north are Mount Mansfield, Belvidere Mountain with the white scar of its asbestos mine, and Owl's Head in Canada. To the east are the Worcester and Granite Mountains and the White Mountains of New Hampshire, including Mount Washington and the Presidential Range, as well as Mount Moosilauke and the Franconia Range. To the west are the Champlain Valley and New York's Adirondack Mountains, and standing alone to the north is Whiteface Mountain.

After you rest and enjoy the scenery, continue north on the Long Trail. The descent is steep on the rocky trail to the hut clearing and the Monroe Trail junction on your right at 4.3 miles. The sign indicates a distance of 3.1 miles back to your car. Take the blue-blazed Monroe Trail, which runs at first steeply and then more moderately downhill, until you reach the yellow-blazed Alpine Trail at 4.9 miles. Continue to descend the Monroe Trail through mixed hard- and softwoods. You cross Camel's Hump Brook at 5.2 miles and soon walk along the base of a large rockface. At 5.4 miles you descend a birch ridge, then hike over rocks that have fallen from the outcrop above you. At 6.1 miles you reach the Monroe/Dean Trail junction and complete your loop. Continue downhill back to the parking area at 7.4 miles.

Note: The Forestry Trail was renamed the Monroe Trail in 1997 to honor trail builder Will S. Monroe, a legendary Long Trail pioneer.

37

Little River History Loop

Total distance: 3.5 miles	
Hiking time: 2½ hours	
Vertical rise: 880 feet	
Rating: Easy to Moderate	
Map: USGS 7.5' Bolton Mountain	

Little River State Park, established in 1962, is an 1100-acre park within 37,000-acre Mount Mansfield State Forest. The park's Waterbury Dam was completed in 1938 by the US Army Corps of Engineers and the Civilian Conservation Corps (CCC) after two serious floods of the Little River in 1927 and 1934.

This hike leads you to abandoned settlements with stone walls, cemeteries, old roads, foundations, orchards, and more. You are welcome to photograph the area and any artifacts you find, but do not remove any items from the park.

How to Get There

Drive west on US 2 from the junction of US 2 and VT 100 (0.0) in Water-bury. At 1.4 miles turn right (north) on the road to the Little River State Park. Go under the interstate and continue to the Waterbury Dam at 4.2 miles. The road bears left, ascends the bank of the dam, and at 4.5 miles reaches the park entrance. A day-use fee is charged. Pass the entry station, and drive down and across a bridge at 5.0 miles. Go past the "Nature Trail" parking area at the bridge, and park in a small lot on the right, across from a gated road.

The Trail

Cross the main road to the park's main entrance at gated Dalley Road. You can pick up a history pamphlet here. Climb gradually uphill along the road-way while listening for the Stevenson Brook. Almost immediately you reach the Hedgehog Hill Trail junction on your right. Turn right off Dalley Road to follow the blue-blazed Hedgehog Hill Trail. At 0.3 mile cross a culvert and begin a short but steep climb. The stone wall indicates old pastures across the roadway. Just ahead at the top of the hill among the pines is a large, flat rock, which is a good place to stop and look over the history pamphlet. This whole area used to be a settlement.

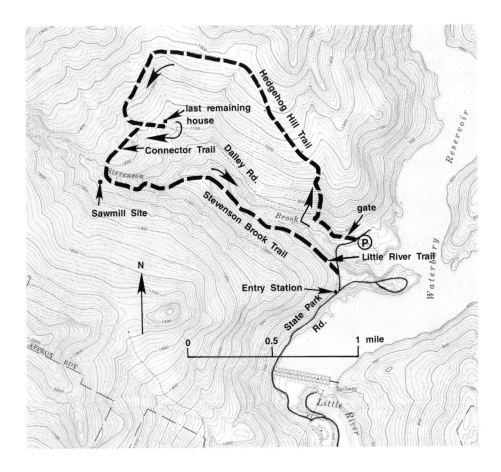

At 0.5 mile you come to an old road and foundation on the left. Numerous old relics are also obvious. Beyond the foundation you follow between two stone walls and wind through white birches until you reach Ricker Cemetery, Site #16. The cemetery is surrounded by white cedar, a species not common in the area. Also known as "arbor vitae," meaning "tree of life," it was planted for symbolic reasons—to give life to the dead.

Beyond the cemetery to the left is a path leading to the former Tom Herbert Farm (#14), which was first settled in 1856. This historical site includes a stand of roses, two cellar holes, and an old well. The well, approximately 50 feet to the southeast of the cellar holes, is 27 feet deep—so be careful.

The trail here is briefly obscured by brush. Keep left to remain on the road until you reach the old Andrew Burley Farm (#13). Most of the foundations are now submerged or obscured by the busy work of beavers. In season, be sure to enjoy the lilac bush and lilies that grow where the house once stood.

Just before a clearing, cross the stone wall and find yourself on the old road again. At 1.0 mile you reach the William Clossey Farm (#12); the

Almeron Goodell place

junction to Kelty Corners enters just beyond. On your right are the remains of the Ricker Mountain School (#11), which was closed in the late 1800s due to a lack of pupils. It reopened in 1908 but was permanently closed in the early 1920s.

Continuing on the main road, you pass the Patterson Trail Junction at 1.3 miles. Just past this intersection on the right is another cemetery up-hill in the woods. Beyond the cemetery the trail begins a long downhill, past an obscure junction, until you reach a major, signed junction at 1.5 miles. Many of these trails are multiuse, so the signs include snow-mobile routes. Disregard the sign saying the sawmill is to the right; instead, turn left at the signpost following the main road. At 1.7 miles you reach the Sawmill Loop junction on your right. You will take this trail, but first keep on the main road, and descend 0.2 mile to the last remaining struc-

ture in the park, the Almeron Goodell Place. This is the only surviving farm-house in the Little River area. Dis-abled Civil War veteran Almeron Goodell was, according to one story, an escaped slave befriended by an area Goodell family. He bought the land around 1864 and built the house of hewn timbers and hand-split shingles.

After exploring the site, hike back uphill to return to the Sawmill Loop Junction at 2.1 miles. Turn left and enter the woods, following old stone walls and across a gully. Again notice the old road and farm implements. Descend to cross a brook on rocks, ascend a steep bank, and reach the junction of the Stevenson Brook Trail at 2.4 miles. A short spur to the right leads to the remains of the Waterbury Last Block Company Sawmill. This steam-powered band sawmill was constructed in 1917 and operated until 1922. The mill, run by two 150-

horsepower boilers, employed 35 men, 44 horse teams, and one truck. The timber was used for ammunition cases and gun stocks, while the finer wood was hauled to Waterbury for cobblers' "lasts" (shoe molds). Now, only the large boiler, truck chassis, and band saws remain.

Return to the junction, making sure to avoid a new snowmobile trail beyond the sawmill. Return along the Stevenson Brook Trail. Past the mill, the trail bears left on an overgrown roadway. During the summer, the first part of the trail is a continuous nettle patch. The old road widens as you descend along Stevenson Brook and reach the abutments of old road bridges. As you walk along the old road, look for evidence of former settlements. You soon enter some hemlocks and reach an overgrown junction where the Little River Trail crosses Stevenson Brook. Continue descending along the right-hand bank of the brook on the Little River Trail. You soon bear to the right and begin to ascend, leaving the brook. At 3.3 miles reach the paved park road; turn left and follow it to your car, at 3.5 miles.

38

Mount Hunger

Total distance: 4 miles

Hiking time: 3½–4 hours

Vertical rise: 2330 feet

Rating: Moderately strenuous

Map: USGS 7.5' Stowe

This hike goes to the open south summit of Mount Hunger, which, at 3539 feet, provides excellent views of the Green Mountain chain and the White Mountains of New Hampshire. Mount Hunger is part of the Worcester chain, which begins near the Winooski River and ends at Elmore Mountain to the north.

How to Get There

Take VT 100 to Waterbury Center and turn east (0.0) on the road to "Waterbury Center P.O./Loomis Hill/Barnes Hill." (This turn is 0.3 mile south of the Cold Hollow Cider Mill.) Drive straight 0.3 mile and turn left (north) onto Maple Street. Just past the fire station, at 0.4 mile, turn right onto Loomis Hill Road, which turns to dirt at 2.3 miles. Bear left at the top of Loomis Hill Road, and continue on Loomis Hill Road until you reach a parking area for 10 to 15 cars on your right at 3.8 miles. A post and sign identify the trailhead, which is also the site where stones were crushed during construction of the interstate.

The Trail

Your pathway begins behind the parking area and passes through the remains of the crusher site. There are no blazes at this point, but the trail is obvious. Blue blazes appear as the trail enters the woods and begins a series of switchbacks through huge, moss-covered boulders. Numerous old logging roads intersect the trail. Cross a gully and resume your climb along a ridge with numerous rock outcrops. At 0.5 mile the trail levels, crosses a small brook, and begins a long climb along a moderate slope.

Look for a large white birch, which indicates the end of the long hill. Turn right and descend along the hillside into a moss-covered, rock-strewn valley that provides cool, welcome relief on a hot summer day.

Cross the valley floor and a small brook. Look for a large boulder field upstream. Continue uphill through

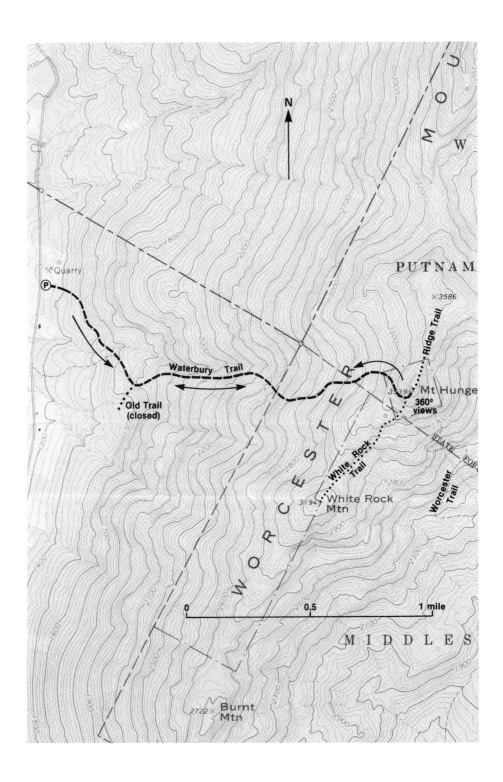

N

Quarry

P

PUTNAM

×3586

Ridge Trail

Waterbury   Trail

Mt Hunge

360°
views

Old Trail
(closed)

White Rock
Trail

WORCESTER

White Rock
Mtn

STATE FOR

Worcester
Trail

MIDDLES

0	0.5	1 mile

Burnt
Mtn

2722

birches until you meet an old trail at 1.0 mile. Turn left, and follow switchbacks up the hillside with several views back into the valley. You soon cross another brook and enter a stand of stately white birches. Climb through the loose rocks and roots until you find a nice large rock on your left at 1.4 miles. This site is a good place to rest. Continue your hike along a more level trail by a brook. The trail enters a hemlock stand and becomes steeper as you pass over large rocks with limited views to the west. At 1.8 miles you reach the junction of the White Rock Trail, which branches to your right.

From the junction continue on the main trail, which steeply ascends a short distance to a view of White Rock Mountain. As you near the summit, you scramble over rocks to the south summit of Mount Hunger. Be sure to avoid the blue-blazed Worcester Trail, which descends the other side of the ridge. Another trail also heads north to the wooded north summit and continues on to Stowe Pinnacle.

The south summit offers spectacular views of Waterbury Reservoir, Camel's Hump, White Rock Mountain, Mount Mansfield, the White Mountains, the Worcester Range, and area valleys. Enjoy the patterns created by the roads, fields, forests, ponds, and rivers below you.

After you rest and enjoy the view, take the same trail back to your car.

39

Stowe Pinnacle

Total distance: 2.8 miles

Hiking time: 2 hours

Vertical rise: 1520 feet

Rating: Moderate

Map: USGS 7.5' Stowe

This short, occasionally steep hike up a rocky knob offers you great views of the entire Worcester Range as well as the Green Mountains, the Waterbury Reservoir, and the surrounding area.

How to Get There
Take VT 100 to the village of Stowe and turn east (0.0) on School Street. At 0.3 mile bear right at the fork on the Stowe Hollow Road. At 1.8 miles the road reaches an intersection, where you go straight on the Upper Hollow Road. The road then crosses a brook. Continue uphill, bear right, pass Pinnacle Road, and at 2.5 miles reach a state parking lot for eight cars on the left (east) side of the road.

The Trail
The blue-blazed trail, which starts at the back of the narrow parking lot, begins by crossing a field and overgrown pasture. Both the Worcester Range and Stowe Pinnacle are directly in front of you. You soon pass by a large boulder and young mixed hardwoods. The trail becomes quite rocky and begins to ascend. At 0.4 mile cross through a gully, turn right, cross another gully, and begin a steeper climb through mature hardwoods. A sharp right turn leads you up onto a plateau. The trail swings left at 0.8 mile, and you scramble over rocks into a notch. As you reach the top of the notch, a short spur trail on your left leads to a view of Mount Mansfield and the Stowe area.

After enjoying the view, return to the junction and follow the main trail behind the ridge you just climbed. The trail descends slightly and then resumes its climb up the pinnacle. As you gain elevation, the trail is rockier, and short fir trees indicate you are nearing the summit. A trail enters from your left that leads to the Worcester Ridge and Hunger Mountain. The Pinnacle Trail bears right, and at 1.4 miles you climb out onto the pinnacle with eastern views of the Worcester Range from Hunger Mountain to

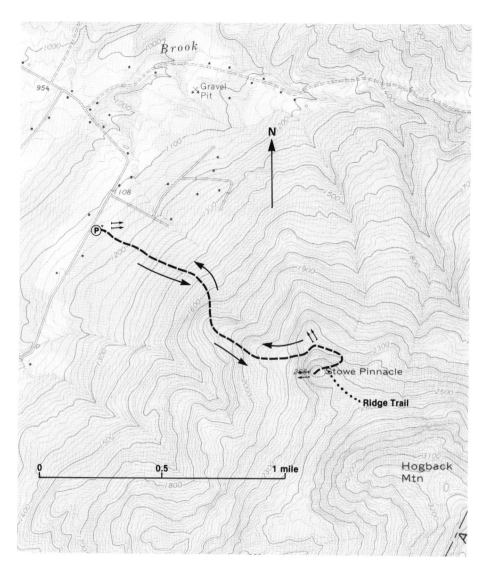

Mount Elmore. There are western views of the Green Mountain range including, from south to north, Mounts Ethan and Ira Allen, Camel's Hump, Bolton Mountain, Mount Mansfield, and Whiteface Mountain. The Waterbury Reservoir can also be seen in the foreground.

Hike back down the same trail to your car.

40

Mount Worcester

Total distance: 5 miles

Hiking time: 3 hours

Vertical rise: 1970 feet

Rating: Moderate

Map: USGS 7.5' Mount Worcester

The Worcester Range parallels the Green Mountains, beginning in Middlesex and ending in Elmore. Its northern terminus is Elmore Mountain; the southern terminus is Mount Hunger. While these two mountains are very popular day hikes and often crowded, Mount Worcester, the central peak from which the ridge derives its name, offers fewer people and excellent views. The trail passes through Putnam State Forest, a collection of approximately 30 parcels of land that have been acquired by the state of Vermont since 1914. Now comprising over 12,000 acres of land, the forest is named for W.R. Putnam, who owned the first two parcels purchased by the state.

How to Get There

The trailhead is reached from the village of Worcester on VT 12 north of Montpelier. Take a left on Minister Brook Road off of VT 12 a short distance north of the Worcester Town Hall (0.0 mile), and follow this road west to Hampshire Hill Road at 1.5 miles.

Turn right on Hampshire Hill Road and follow it uphill. At 3.7 miles you pass Hancock Brook Road on the right. Immediately after crossing Hancock Brook itself (on a culvert, just past the road junction), turn left onto a narrow lane that parallels the brook. Bear right onto a narrow logging road (with a trail sign) by a mobile home. The logging road goes behind a house and forks. Take the left-hand fork to the trailhead at 4.1 miles.

The Trail

Although there is only a "Putnam State Forest" sign, the Mount Worcester trail begins at the old logging road beyond the five-car parking area. For the first section, the trail follows an old logging road, crosses a small brook, then bears right at a fork. You can hear a brook in the valley on your left as you ascend at 0.3 mile. As you cross the brook you have been hearing, keep your eyes open—moose are often seen in this area!

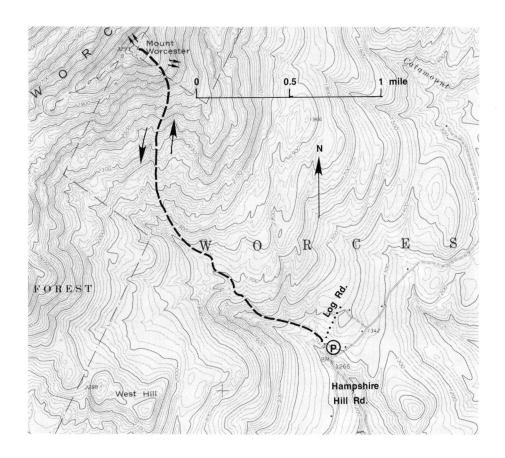

At 0.6 mile you come to an unusual upside-down, furnace-shaped metal object with carrying rings.

By 0.9 mile the brook you have been paralleling becomes quite small, although several picturesque cascades appear as the trail pitch increases. You soon pass a split-rock outcrop—a good resting spot, complete with a view of the cascades. After crossing the brook, hike through a stand of birches and ascend the trail, which becomes muddy and steep. At 2.0 miles you reach a plateau, and the forest changes to mountain ash—trees distinguished by their bright orange berries.

The trail climbs steeply out of the plateau past rock outcrops at 2.2 miles.

You reach a col (a saddlelike depression in a ridge), follow the ridge for a short distance, then bear sharply to the left and begin a long rock scramble. As the trees get smaller and the view opens up at 2.3 miles, look behind you. You will see Mount Washington among the White Mountains of New Hampshire to the east. Be careful to note the trail location in this section as blazes are scarce along the rocks and scrub brush. One notable feature to look for is a layer of quartz in the rock as you ascend. You reach the 3286-foot summit at 2.5 miles.

Several different points on the summit offer excellent views and protection from the weather. Moving around to the various points allows you to

Mount Worcester summit

get a 360-degree view. To the west, Stowe Pinnacle is below you, with Mount Mansfield the prominent summit beyond; to the north is Mount Elmore; and to the south is the Worcester Range with Camel's Hump in the distance.

After you have rested and enjoyed the views, hike back down the same trail to your car.

41

Elmore Mountain and Balanced Rock

Total distance: 4.5 miles

Hiking time: 3 hours

Vertical rise: 1470 feet

Rating: Moderate

Map: USGS 7.5' Morrisville

Good views, a refurbished fire tower, old stone foundations, a glacial boulder, and a beautiful lake at the foot of the mountain make this hike a wonderful choice for a day of outdoor activities in Elmore State Park.

The park, which charges a day-use fee, was established in 1933 when the town of Elmore deeded approximately 30 acres of land, including the beach on Lake Elmore, to the state. During the early 1940s, the Civilian Conservation Corps (CCC) constructed the bathhouse, a picnic area, and a summit fire tower and caretaker's cabin. The only public recreational facility in Lamoille County, the 706-acre park offers access to camping, a picnic area, hiking trails, swimming, boating, fish-

ing, hunting, snowmobiling, cross-country skiing, and a winter weekend of dogsled racing. Lake Elmore is 204 acres in size and averages 8 feet deep, with a maximum depth of 15 feet. The lake is classified as a fair to good warm-water fishing area. The most-sought-after fish in Lake Elmore is northern pike, although an abundant perch population has limited the numbers of other species. Little Elmore Pond upstream has better quality fishing and is annually stocked with brown trout. While most of the park is forested, the steep terrain limits the availability of commercial timber.

How to Get There
Elmore State Park is located on VT 12 in Elmore. From the park entrance, drive left past the booth and into the woods. Follow the winding gravel road uphill 0.6 mile through the picnic area to a turn-around and parking area at the end of the road by the gate.

The Trail
Your pathway starts at the gate and continues on the gravel road. Follow this road to the top of the first grade, where a short spur on your right leads to a beaver pond. Continue on the

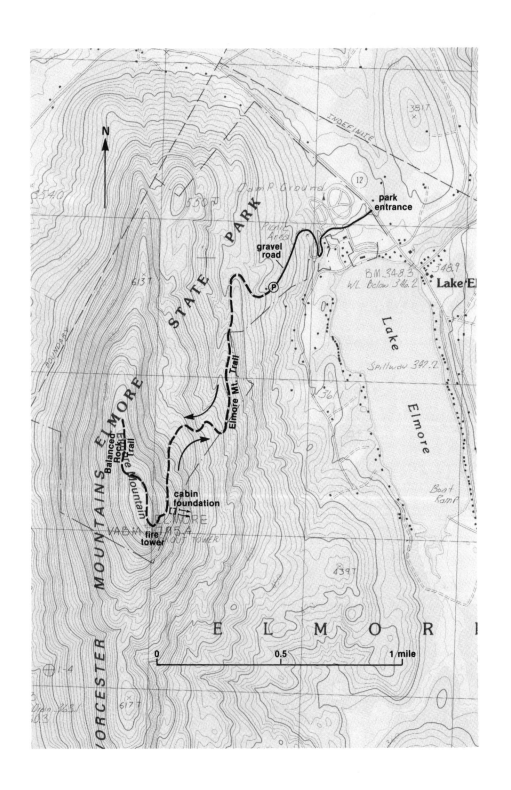

N

INDEFINITE

CampGround

park
entrance

Picnic
Area

gravel
road

P

BM 348.3
W.L. below 346.2

348.9

Lake El

STATE   PARK

ELMORE

613 T

Lake

540

560 T

BOUNDARY

Spillway 347.2

Elmore

361

Elmore Mt. Trail

Balanced
Rock
Trail

Mountain

cabin
foundation

ELMORE
1165.4
LOOKOUT TOWER

VABM

fire
tower

Boat
Ramp

3817

12

MOUNTAINS

WORCESTER

4397

E   L   M   O   R   E

617 T

0   0.5   1 /mile

1-4

Drain 363.1
103

View from Elmore Mountain

road past a rock cut and then uphill to the end of the gravel road at 0.5 mile. At this point the trail makes a sharp right turn, climbs the road bank on steps, and enters the woods. Follow a gully uphill with a small brook to your right as the trail ascends with occasional views of the lake on your left. Be sure to avoid the many spur trails in this section.

At 0.9 mile you switch back to the right and immediately make two steep ascents. At the top of the second ascent, pass through a rock cut and continue over more level terrain. Next, cross a small brook on two logs, swing left, and ascend again. As you follow this gully upward, the trail looks very steep ahead. Don't worry—the trail bears left and begins a series of sweeping uphill switchbacks.

As you ascend the last long climb, white birches appear ahead. At 1.4 miles you enter a clearing, the former site of the fire warden's cabin, which was destroyed by an arsonist in 1982. All that remains is the foundation and chimney, yet the flowers planted by the warden near the foundation continue to bloom each spring and summer. From the clearing you have a good view down to the lake and the White Mountains to the east.

Continue your hike behind the cabin's site, and begin your final climb to the summit. Be careful not to slip into the spring, the original supply of water for the ranger's cabin. The summit climb is best described as a very steep scramble over rocks and roots!

At 1.7 miles you reach the junction of the Balanced Rock Trail, noted by a blue arrow and "B.R." painted on a rock. Stay on the main trail, and continue your hike a short distance to the tower, which is in excellent condition. It ceased to be used as a fire tower in the fall of 1974 but was repainted and repaired in 1987 by the state of Vermont.

Spectacular views from the tower include the Worcester Range to the south as well as the entire Green Mountain range north from Camel's Hump, including Mount Mansfield, Laraway Mountain, Mount Belvidere (with its asbestos mine "scar"), and Jay Peak. To the west is the White Mountain chain from Mount Moosilauke to Mount Washington. The tower is also used by bird watchers every spring and fall, during hawk migrations.

After resting and enjoying the views, return to the Balanced Rock junction, and follow this side trail along Elmore's ridge to a rock outcrop with beautiful views. The trail swings up and away from the east outcrop, climbs a shelf, and continues northwest over the ridge to a western outcrop. Follow along the ridge to the north behind the outcrop, descend slightly, and reach another outcrop with deep cracks created when weathered rock plates slid off the mountain. Be sure to enjoy the impressive views through these cracks. At 2.25 miles you reach Balanced Rock, a boulder left perched on the ridge by a glacier that receded during the last Ice Age.

Hike back to the junction and down the trail to your car. After completing your hike, cool off and refresh yourself with a swim in beautiful Lake Elmore. The lake is also a favorite site for local windsurfers; you may be able to rent a windsurfing board and give it a try.

42

Mount Mansfield

Total distance: 9.3 miles

Hiking time: 2 days, 1 night

Vertical rise: 3825 feet

*Rating: Day 1—difficult,
Day 2—moderate*

Maps: USGS 7.5' Mansfield

Mount Mansfield, elevation 4393 feet, is the highest mountain in Vermont and a National Landmark. Because the mountain resembles the profile of a human face when viewed from the east, distinctive points on the ridge are called—south to north—the Forehead, Nose, Upper Lip, Lower Lip, Chin, and Adam's Apple. The Abenakis called the mountain "Mose-o-de-be Waso," which means "Mountain-with-the-head-of-a-moose." Europeans probably named the mountain for the town of Mansfield, which was disestablished more than 100 years ago.

The summit ridge of Mount Mansfield supports a rare and beautiful arctic-alpine plant community. Many of these rare and fragile plants look like common grass and are difficult to distinguish, so please remember to

stay on the trails and rock outcrops.

To learn more about this interesting environment, talk to one of the ranger-naturalists stationed on Mount Mansfield during the hiking season. They are there through the cooperation of the University of Vermont, the Mount Mansfield Company, the Vermont Department of Forests, Parks and Recreation, and the Green Mountain Club. (Also see "Arctic-Alpine Vegetation" in the introduction.)

The ridge of Mount Mansfield, owned by the University of Vermont, attracts over 40,000 hikers each year and is included in the Vermont Fragile Areas Registry. While many people prefer direct routes to the top via the toll road and Gondola, there are no fewer than 9 approach trails to the summit ridge, over 15 other trails along the ridgeline, and 31 trails in the Mansfield area.

You begin your first day ascending Mount Mansfield from Smuggler's Notch Road to Taft Lodge, a distance of 1.7 miles. Unlike a day hike, a backpacking trip allows you to explore more of the mountain's special points of interest, like Adam's Apple, Lake of the Clouds, and the Chin. In case you decide to leave your backpack at Taft Lodge (see page 173) while you ex-

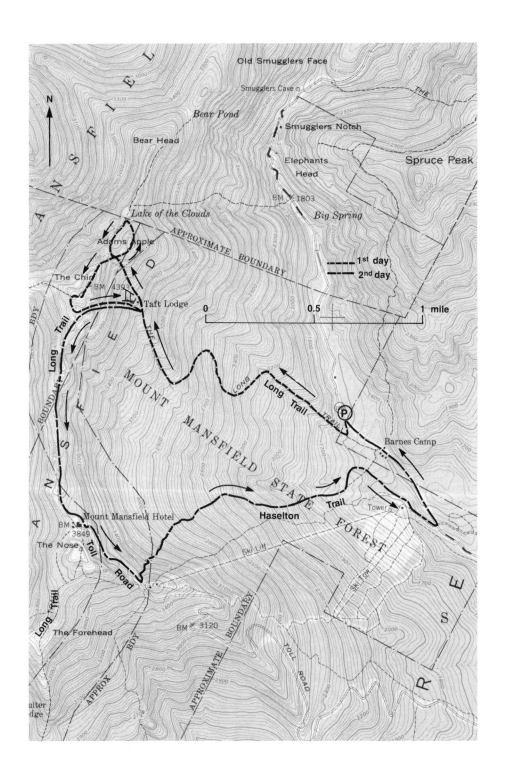

plore, bring a day pack with you.

How to Get There

Take VT 108 (the Stowe-Jeffersonville Highway) to the Long Trail parking area on the south side of VT 108 just before the picnic area. The 10- to 15-car parking lot is 0.7 mile from the Mount Mansfield Ski Area, 8.5 miles north of Stowe, or 9.5 miles south of Jeffersonville.

The Trail

Day One

Total distance: 3.9 miles
Hiking time: 5 hours
Vertical rise: 2995 feet

Hike south from the parking area on VT 108 to the Long Trail trailhead, which includes an information board with distances to various points on the mountain. Ascend the steep bank, hike parallel to the highway, and bear right on easier grades through a beech and yellow birch forest. Notice the extensive trail work of steps and water bars built over the years by the Green Mountain Club to slow the impact of heavy trail use.

Follow along a brook, then zigzag uphill until you reach a registration box. Bear right up a set of stairs, hike over rolling terrain, and cross a small brook twice. Continue your ascent with possible views of Elephants Head, a great cliff on the east side of the notch.

A series of switchbacks brings you along a ski trail at 1.1 miles, where you can see the Nose and summit towers. Bear right and ascend the sometimes quite steep trail. To your right you can see Spruce Peak Ski Area and Madonna Mountain. Begin a very steep ascent until you reach Taft Lodge at 1.7 miles. This log cabin, the largest and oldest shelter on the Long Trail, was built in 1920, then rebuilt in 1996 by Green Mountain Club and other volunteers under the direction of Fred Gilbert. It has bunk space for 32 people. A GMC caretaker is in residence during the hiking season and a small fee is charged for overnight use. Due to the area's fragile nature, tent camping is not permitted, and there are special policies for waste disposal. Please follow all instructions while at the lodge.

Since Taft Lodge is your day one destination, you may choose to leave your backpack there and continue your exploration of the mountain with a lighter day pack. If you make the switch, bring along some food, water, a first-aid kit, and extra clothes. Remember that weather conditions can change quite rapidly on the summit. Continue up the mountain to a trail junction at Eagle Pass at 2.0 miles. Bear right at the junction on the Adam's Apple Trail, which ascends to the open summit of the Adam's Apple. To the south you will see the steep wall of the Chin. Before hiking to the Chin, continue north ascending the Adam's Apple Trail toward Lake of the Clouds, the highest lake in Vermont. At the junction of the Hell Brook and Bear Pond Trails, turn left on the Hell Brook Trail around the Adam's Apple, and return to Eagle Pass at 2.4 miles. At Eagle Pass continue south on the Long Trail, and ascend the steep face of the Chin to the summit of Mount Mansfield at 2.7 miles. Remember to stay on the marked trails and rock outcrops to avoid disturbing the fragile alpine vegetation and thin mountain soils. Many of these protected plants look like ordinary grass and are easily damaged by stray footsteps.

From the Chin you have an extensive 360-degree view. To the northeast are the Sterling Range, Laraway Moun-

Former Mount Mansfield Summit House

tain, the Cold Hollow Mountains, Belvidere Mountain, Big Jay, Jay Peak, and the Pinnacle in Canada. To the east are the Worcester Mountains and, beyond them, the Granite Mountains and peaks of the Northeast Kingdom. To the southeast are Mount Washington in New Hampshire and the White Mountains south of the Connecticut Lakes. To the south are the Green Mountains as far south as Killington Peak. To the west are the Adirondack Mountains of New York, including Whiteface Mountain and Mount Marcy. To the northwest you can sometimes see Mount Royal and the skyscrapers in Montreal on a clear day.

After resting and enjoying the spectacular view, continue south along the summit. Hike past the Profanity and Sunset Ridge Trails to the junction of the Subway Trail at 3.0 miles on the west side of the ridge. Although fun and exciting, the Subway Trail is extremely difficult and should *not* be attempted with a full backpack or in

bad weather. The rocks are extremely slippery when wet. Steeply descend the western face of the mountain through a rock fall area. Agile maneuvering is required around the caves, crevices, and boulders.

After passing through the Subway and ascending a ladder, you quickly return to the ridge on the Subway and Canyon North Extension Trail at 3.3 miles. Back on the ridge, turn left (north), and hike along the Long Trail to the Profanity Trail junction at 3.4 miles. Turn right on the Profanity Trail, and steeply descend to Taft Lodge at 3.9 miles.

Day Two

Total distance: 5.4 miles

Hiking time: 3½ to 4 hours

Vertical rise: 830 feet

After a good night's rest, return to the summit at 0.5 mile with your backpack via the Profanity Trail. Hike along the ridgeline past a large rock cairn, called Frenchman's Pile, which marks the site where a hiker was killed by lightning many years ago. If you are caught on the mountain during a thunderstorm, leave the ridge and crouch upon loose rocks that are not immersed in standing water. Do not sit or lie upon the ground or touch the soil with your hands because ground currents may travel through your chest. Avoid exposed trees and rock outcrops. Caves and shallow overhangs are dangerous because ground currents jump through these gaps after a strike.

When you reach the top of the Toll Road and the Summit Station at 1.7 miles, leave your pack on the rocks and climb up the Nose for a parting look at the ridge you have just hiked. Return to the Summit Station at 2.1 miles.

The parking lot at the top of the road was the site of the old Mount Mansfield Summit House, which was one of New England's most successful summit hotels until 1958. In 1862, the poet and essayist Ralph Waldo Emerson wrote that "a man went through the house ringing a large bell and shouting 'Sunrise,'" every morning. Vigorous guests rolled out of bed and climbed the Nose for a pre-breakfast sunrise view.

From the summit station, begin your descent down the Toll Road to the Nose Dive Ski Trail, a former ski racecourse, at 2.3 miles. Descend the ski trail, and look for a trail sign on the left for the Haselton Trail. This trail, one of the oldest on the mountain, is named for Judge Seneca Haselton, the first vice-president of the Green Mountain Club. Continue your descent on the Haselton Trail to the Gondola Base Station at 4.4 miles. Follow the access road down to VT 108, turn left, and hike back to your car at 5.4 miles.

43

Sterling Pond and Elephants Head

Total distance: 6.5-mile loop

Hiking time: 4 hours

Vertical rise: 1780 feet

Rating: Strenuous

Map: USGS 7.5' Mount Mansfield

This trail begins in Smugglers Notch, a beautiful passageway between Mount Mansfield and Sterling Peak. Smugglers Notch was a favorite route for smuggling goods into and out of Canada. In 1807, northern Vermonters faced a serious hardship when President Jefferson passed an embargo act. The act forbade American trade with Great Britain and Canada. Because Montreal was such a close and lucrative market, many Vermonters continued illegal trade with Canada by herding cattle and transporting other goods through the notch. The notch was also used by fugitive slaves as an escape route to Canada and by Vermonters in the 1920s to smuggle liquor from Canada during Prohibition.

The rocks of the notch were formed about 400 million years ago when the land was at the bottom of a shallow sea. Clay particles, sand, and animal shells drifted to the sea floor and eventually were pressed into shale-type rocks. About 100 million years later, the land was pushed up to form the Green Mountains. The sedimentary rocks were subjected to tremendous pressure and high temperatures, which rearranged the minerals into the banded patterns you see today. This "metamorphosed" rock, called schist, is primarily composed of the minerals mica, albite, and quartz, and occasionally garnet, magnetite, and chlorite.

Although geologists are not certain how the notch was formed, most believe that it was carved by a southward-flowing river. Twelve thousand years ago, as the first glacier was retreating, the ice on the eastern side of the Green Mountains probably melted first. The glacier remained on the western side and blocked the meltwater from flowing west. Thus, a river of melted ice rushed through the notch, down into the Stowe area.

The magnificent cliffs of the notch contain shapes that resemble people

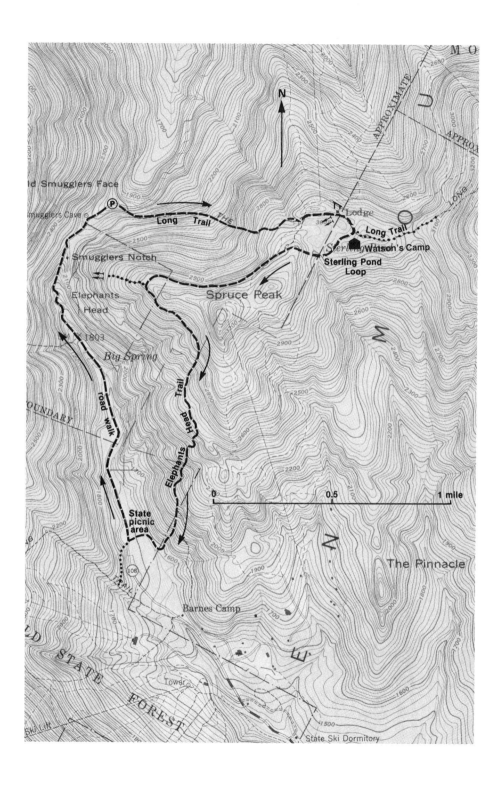

N

Old Smugglers Face

Smugglers Cave

Long Trail

THE

Lodge

Long Trail

Love

Sterling Watson's Camp

Smugglers Notch

Elephants Head

1803

Big Spring

Sterling Pond Loop

Spruce Peak

road walk

BOUNDARY

Elephants Head Trail

State picnic area

108

0   0.5   1 mile

The Pinnacle

TRAIL

OLD STATE FOREST

Barnes Camp

Tower

Ski Lift

State Ski Dormitory

Sterling Pond

or animals. With a little imagination you can find the Smuggler's Face, Singing Bird, Elephants Head, and Hunter and His Dog. The cliffs also contain some of the rarest and most endangered plants in Vermont. The constantly dripping water in the cliff's cracks breaks down the rock minerals and nourishes the few plants that manage to grow in the cracks. The combination of a steep face where few plants can survive, a cold microclimate, and a constant supply of mineral-rich water creates a very unusual set of environmental factors. This plant community is called a cold calcareous cliff community. Please take extreme care to neither disturb nor pick any plants in the notch.

How to Get There

To reach Smuggler's Notch, take VT 108, the Stowe-Jeffersonville Highway, 10 miles north of Stowe or 8 miles south of Jeffersonville. Park in the lot at the top of the notch.

The Trail

Before you begin your hike, be sure to review the information on the parking area bulletin board. A short distance to the left of the parking area and information booth is Smuggler's Cave, an alleged hiding place for smuggled goods during the War of 1812.

From the parking area, cross the road and take the white-blazed Long Trail north. There is another information board at the beginning of the trail. Start your hike up a steep ascent on stone steps, across a drainage gully, and along a plateau. To the left are views down the steep bank into the notch, and ahead is a large rock outcrop. The trail ascends steeply to the right. A log bench at the top provides a welcome spot to rest.

Continue your climb on moderate to steep grades up the hillside, through softwoods and a series of plateaus with occasional views along the way. At 0.8 mile you reach a ski trail that connects the Sterling and Spruce Peak lifts. Turn left, and follow the wide ski trail down to the outlet of Sterling Pond. You can see Madonna Mountain across the pond.

Surrounded by boreal forest, Sterling Pond is spring fed, stocked with trout, and relatively shallow, although beaver dams have increased the depth of the pond. Originally a large talc deposit, the pond formed after the last glacier cut a depression in the talc. There are still talc deposits along the trail. Watch your step; they're very slippery. At one time, a talc mine was considered, but it was disregarded because the pond was too remote.

Watch your footing as you cross the pond outlet and ascend the bare rock face just past the pond. After continuing through the woods for a short distance, the Long Trail crosses a ski trail at 1.0 mile. The trail then reenters the woods and reaches Sterling Pond Shelter at 1.2 miles. (Due to the popularity of the area, a Green Mountain Club caretaker is stationed at Sterling Pond during the hiking season.) Take time to enjoy the great view of Mount Mansfield across the pond.

While at the shelter, notice that the white-blazed Long Trail—which you do not take—continues behind the shelter. Your hike follows the blue-blazed spur trail that passes around the pond to Watson's Camp, once a private camp, which was donated to the Green Mountain Club by Thomas J. Watson in 1980. From the camp, follow the blue-blazed Elephant's Head Trail, which passes below the camp and along the shoreline of Sterling Pond. Be careful because the trail can be very wet near the pond.

Leaving the pond, the trail ascends a steep knoll and at 2.0 miles reaches a ski trail that connects Spruce Peak Ski Area and Sterling Pond. Go straight across the ski trail and reenter the woods. Swing west around Spruce Peak, and enjoy good views across the notch. Watch your step as you hike down a series of very steep pitches.

At 2.7 miles you reach the spur trail to the top of Elephants Head. Turn right on the spur trail and begin a steep descent to the top of Elephants Head at 2.8 miles. From the cliff summit, you can see 1000 feet straight down to the roadway below. Across the notch are the sheer walls of Mount Mansfield and the scar left by the 1983 landslide.

Because peregrine falcons have recently returned to the Elephants Head cliff, the trail to the top of Elephants Head may be closed during their nesting season. These beautiful, endangered birds are extremely sensitive to human disturbance, especially from above. Please obey all trail signs during nesting season, which runs from February through mid-July, and see the introduction for more information about the falcons.

Follow the spur trail back to the main trail, and turn right at the junction. The trail becomes quite steep as you hike and sometimes crawl up and down the hillside on exposed rocks and roots. Be very careful of your footing. Expect to lower yourself occasionally over rock outcrops. This trail is very rugged but quite beautiful and worth the extra effort.

The trail begins a switchback to the right as birches appear and the grade becomes easier. As you cross the 1985 rock and mud slide at 3.8 miles, notice how thin the soils are along the slide at this elevation. Enter the woods, complete another long switchback, and cross the lower portion of the slide. Continue downhill on more moderate grades through a mixed forest of birch and maple. The trail narrows, passes over a rock ledge at 4.3 miles, and soon gets steep again. Descend a long grade, swing right, and cross two brooks. Pass by the picnic area outhouse, and turn right to the picnic area at 4.5 miles.

Continue your hike along VT 108, through the notch, and back to the parking area. Along the way, observe the lower portion of the slide you previously crossed. At 5.8 miles you reach Big Spring, a nice place to stop for a well-deserved drink. Hike through the hairpin turns and among the boulders, which have fallen into the notch, back to your car at 6.5 miles.

44

Mount Pisgah

Total distance: 2.5 miles

Hiking time: 2–2½ hours

Vertical rise: 1590 feet

Rating: Moderate

Map: USGS 7.5' Sutton Provisional

Mount Pisgah and Mount Hor (see Hike 45) are located on Lake Willoughby and form the sheer cliffs that descend to the lake. The cliffs have been designated a National Natural Landmark as well as a Natural Area by the state of Vermont. Approximately 993 acres of the area are permanently protected. The geologic formation of Lake Willoughby and the adjacent cliffs area are unique, and there are different interpretations of the formation process. The lake lies in a trough cut in the granite by an exceptionally fine example of glacial scouring. Development, timber cutting, and road building are prohibited within the natural area.

The mountains are located in the 7300-acre Willoughby State Forest, which was established in 1928. Much of the original purchase was once open

farmland. In the 1930s the Civilian Conservation Corps established plantations of Norway and white spruce as well as red and white pine. The forest includes hiking, cross-country skiing, and snowmobile trails, and six small cold-water ponds are annually stocked with brook and rainbow trout. Deer and grouse hunting are also popular within the forest.

Most of the trails in the area are still maintained by the Westmore Association and its associated Trails Committee. Although the association formed in 1967, some of the Westmore trails were laid out long before that time. Maintained by the association until 1989, the Mount Pisgah trails and the Mount Hor Trail (Hawkes Trail—see Hike 45) are now maintained by the state of Vermont.

Mount Pisgah is located on the east side of Lake Willoughby. The trail parallels a steep rock face with great views down to the lake, Burke Mountain, and the surrounding area. The original "south" trail up Pisgah dates back to the late 1800s.

How to Get There

To reach the Mount Pisgah trailhead from the south, start from the intersection of US 5 and VT 5A in West

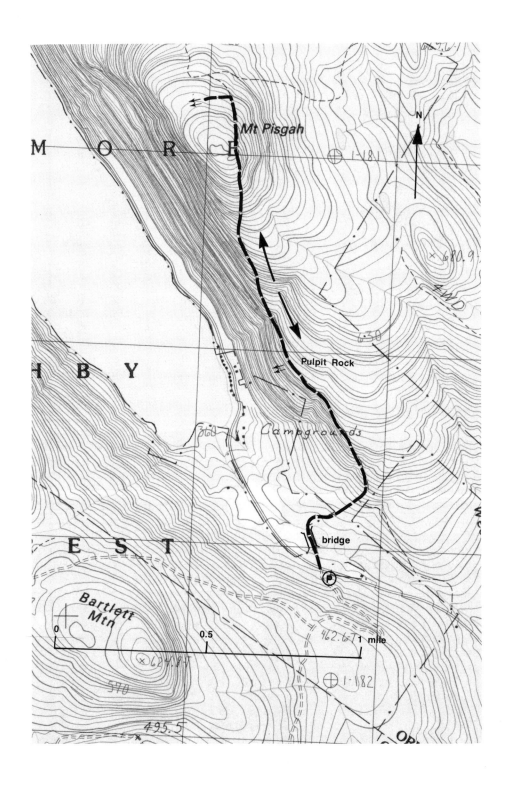

Mt Pisgah

N

MORE

HBY

Pulpit Rock

Campgrounds

EST

bridge

Ⓟ

Bartlett Mtn

0   0.5   1 mile

Burke (0.0), and drive 5.7 miles north to the parking area on the left (west) side of the road before Lake Willoughby.

To reach the trailhead from the north or east, drive east on VT 16 from the center of Barton (0.0) to the intersection of VT 16 and VT 5 at 0.3 mile. Turn left on VT 16, and continue to the VT 5A intersection at 7.3 miles. Turn right (south) on VT 5A to the parking area on the right (west) side of the road at 13.0 miles. As you drive along the east side of Lake Willoughby, you can see Mount Hor on the right and Mount Pisgah on the left.

The parking area for 20 cars has picnic tables for a lunch or snack, plus a signboard about the area trails. The trailhead sign on the opposite side of the road indicates a distance of 1.7 miles to the summit of Mount Pisgah.

The Trail

Cross the road and descend the road embankment on the blue-blazed trail until you come to a swamp. Avoid the faint blue blazes to your right. Instead, turn left and cross a wooden bridge over the swamp. You can see occasional views of the Mount Hor cliffs. Climb the bank behind the pond, and follow an old road that bears right away from the pond.

As you start to see a clearing ahead, the trail makes a sharp left and begins a long switchback climb. Look for a water pipe along the trail, and take time to notice the extensive maintenance work required in this area. You soon follow the ridge uphill on a wide, more gradual trail. To the left is the steep side of the mountain descending to Lake Willoughby. At 0.9 mile a small sign indicates the spur trail to Pulpit Rock, where you have an excellent view down to the lake and of Mount Hor beyond. Be careful—you are standing on a rock overhang, approximately 650 feet above the lake.

Back on the main trail, continue a steady climb along the ridge, and then bear right. Moving away from the lake, you enter a maple forest, ascend the hillside, and hike through a birch forest. As the trail gets narrower, climb through boulders and skirt a ledge at 1.3 mile. You have now lost all views of the lake as you enter a softwood forest along the backside of the mountain.

The trail switches back until you find yourself at the bottom of a long rock slab. Climb the slab for a good view of the Burke Mountain area. Above the slab, you enter the woods and reach a side trail leading to East Overlook. Continue down along the ridge until, at 1.9 miles, you reach a spur trail on your left to the Upper Overlook. Take this steep, muddy trail down to a spectacular view of Lake Memphremagog, Lake Willoughby, Wheeler Mountain, Mount Hor, Jay Peak, the Green Mountain Range, and the surrounding area.

Return to the trail junction and hike back down the main trail to your car.

45

Mount Hor

Total distance: 3.5 miles

Hiking time: 3 hours

Vertical rise: 1050 feet

Rating: Easy to moderate

Map: USGS 7.5′ Sutton

Mount Hor is located to the west of Lake Willoughby (see Hike 44 for information on Willoughby State Forest). The summit is wooded, but the trail goes to two vantage points on the cliffs, with beautiful views of the lake below. The Mount Hor Trail is now called the Herbert and Evelyn Hawkes Trail in honor of two members of the Westmore Association who laid out the trail to the mountain summit and overlook.

How to Get There

To reach the Mount Hor trailhead, follow the directions to the Mount Pisgah parking area (Hike 44), then proceed up the narrow gravel road at the right side of the parking area (0.0). Bear right at the fork. Continue up the road to a small parking area for five cars on your right at 1.8 miles.

The Trail

A sign just past the parking area on the right side of the road marks the blue-blazed trail up Mount Hor. Climb the bank and follow an old road to your right. There are very few blazes on the small maple trees, so be careful to stay on the trail.

At 0.4 mile you begin a hillside walk through maples and nettles. As you approach the top of the maple grove, the trail swings left and across a series of switchbacks until you reach a trail junction at 0.7 mile.

From this junction, hike uphill on the serpentine, overgrown, and only faintly blazed West Branch Trail to the wooded summit of Mount Hor. Just beyond the summit is an overlook of Bean, Wheeler, Blake, Duck, and Vail Ponds as well as Burke Mountain.

Return to the trail junction, and follow the East Branch/Wheeler Pond Trail along the ridge line to the overlooks above Lake Willoughby. You soon reach a trail junction. Do not take the Wheeler Pond Trail, which turns left and descends 5 miles to the pond. Continue on the East Branch Trail along the ridge to the junction of East Lookout Trail on your right. Descend on the East Lookout Trail to

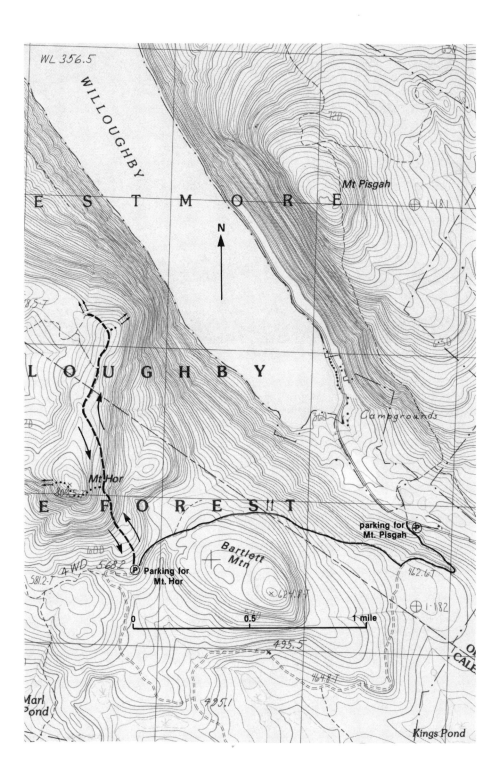

WL 356.5

WILLOUGHBY

WESTMORE

N

Mt Pisgah

⊕ 1·181

LOUGHBY

Campgrounds

Mt Hor

E FOREST

parking for
Mt. Pisgah ⊕

Bartlett
Mtn

962.6-T

4WD 568.2

Ⓟ Parking for
Mt. Hor

581.2-T

×2648-T

⊕ 1·182

0   0.5   1 mile

495.5

464.8-T

Marl
Pond

495.1

Kings Pond

OL
CALE

Multizoned polystictus—also known as turkey tails

an overlook of the lake. An even better lookout is found by going a little farther down the ridge to the north lookout, which overlooks Lake Willoughby and Mount Pisgah beyond. This lookout, with its breathtaking views, is a breezy place to stop for lunch.

Return to the summit to hike back down to the trailhead.

46

Prospect Rock (Johnson)

Total distance: 2 miles	
Hiking time: 1½ hours	
Vertical rise: 540 feet	
Rating: Easy	
Map: USGS 7.5′ Johnson	

This short hike offers superb views, including Whiteface Mountain and the Lamoille River as it meanders through the valley below and empties into Lake Champlain.

Before or after your hike be sure to take the short walk through the woods by the parking area to view the Lamoille River and Ithiel Falls, a set of Class 2 rapids where the river narrows between two cliffs.

How To Get There

From Johnson (0.0), drive west on VT 15 to the Lamoille River bridge at 1.5 miles. Just before the bridge, turn right (north) on Hogback Road, and continue to a five-car parking area at 2.2 miles on your left at the top of the hill.

The Trail

From the parking area follow the paved road northwest 0.1 mile to the Ithiel Falls Camp meeting grounds. Ithiel Falls Camp is a religious family camp with a series of cabins and buildings. Turn right, and follow the white-blazed Long Trail up the gravel road opposite the cabins and past a rock outcrop. Halfway up the bank a small sign indicates an incorrect trail length of 0.6 mile to Prospect Rock. Remnants of old cabins from the camp are seen along the short gravel road. Please remember that you are on private property, and should respect all lands and buildings.

The trail soon turns left off the gravel road and enters the woods, where a new sign indicates a correct distance of 0.8 mile to the Prospect Rock overlook.

Cross a small brook and ascend to another brook. Now following an old logging road, the trail zigzags up the hill. At 0.4 mile you cross a wet area on puncheon, and return to the old road.

Large boulders line the trail as you hike on almost level ground through a forest of mixed hard- and softwoods. Climb along steep switchbacks, and then ascend more gently until you

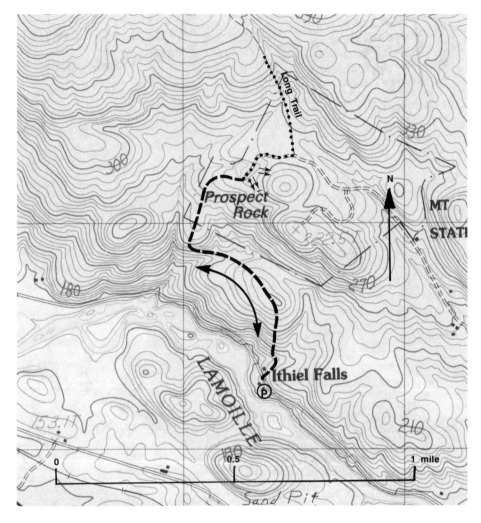

see the end of the Prospect Rock out-crop and enter an area filled with ferns and raspberry bushes.

At 0.8 mile the trail makes a sharp right, ascends the steep hillside, then levels off and opens up onto Prospect Rock. Avoid the numerous spur trails as you head onto the rocks. After enjoying the spectacular views of Whiteface Mountain, Daniel's Notch, and the Lamoille River Valley below, hike back down the trail to your car.

47

Ritterbush Camp and Devil's Gulch

Total distance: 5 miles

Hiking time: 3 hours

Vertical rise: 1040 feet

Rating: Moderate

Maps: USGS 15' Hyde Park and 15' Jay Peak

This pleasant half-day hike takes you to Devil's Gulch, Ritterbush Camp, and Ritterbush Pond. Portions of the Long Trail in this area were recently acquired by the State of Vermont. More than 10 miles of the Long Trail south from Ritterbush Pond, including Devil's Gulch, are now protected under state ownership through the efforts of The Nature Conservancy and the Green Mountain Club.

How to Get There
Look for a metal Long Trail sign on VT 118 between Eden and Belvidere Corners at the height-of-land. The trailhead is approximately 4.9 miles from the VT 100/118 junction in Eden.

Park on the wide shoulder or in the four-car parking area on the north side of the road.

The Trail
From VT 118 follow the Long Trail south, up a bank, until you reach a registration box. Be sure to register, and then continue your hike through overgrown farm pasture. After a short ascent, you reach a power-line cut with a view toward the east and VT 118. In the summer the fields and cleared power-line cut are filled with a variety of beautiful wildflowers.

Continue through a gully of young hardwoods, and begin a steep but short climb until you crest the ridge at 0.5 mile. The forest opens up from past logging activities as you hike uphill on a logging road through ferns and hardwoods. At 0.9 mile you begin a slight descent through more mixed hardwoods until you reach an overlook to Ritterbush Pond, a deep glacial cirque (steep-walled mountain basin), at 1.5 miles.

The pond is part of the Babcock Nature Preserve, a natural area created in 1974. This tract of undeveloped wilderness was given to the Vermont State Colleges through The

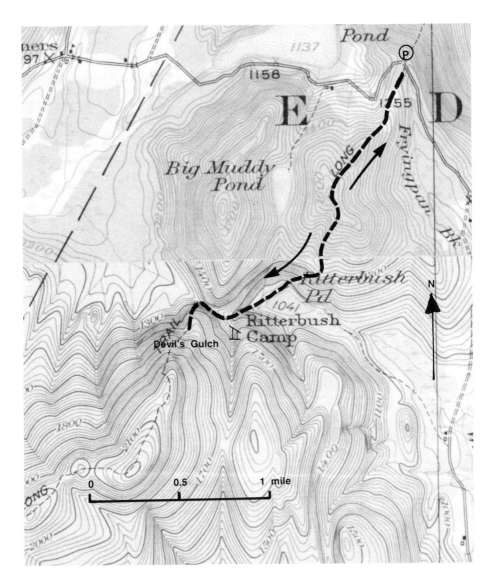

Nature Conservancy by Robert S. Babcock and includes 1030 acres of mature, minimally disturbed, deciduous and mixed woodland with numerous streams, meadows, and three permanent ponds. Wildlife in the preserve includes the pygmy shrew (the world's smallest mammal), bobcat, bear, and moose. The preserve is also a prime birding location and the northernmost breeding locale of the Louisiana waterthrush. Big Muddy and Ritterbush Ponds, as well as adjacent lands, are part of a watershed and a 3-year, nationally funded research study of forest nutrient dynamics and acid rain impact. Administration of the preserve is handled by Johnson State College.

Continuing your hike, follow the trail that bears right at the overlook, begins a long steep descent utilizing log and stone steps, and parallels the edge of the hillside. At 1.9 miles you cross two small brooks and pass a spur trail on your right to Big Muddy Pond. Continue on the Long Trail over rolling terrain until you reach the edge of a long outcrop. Follow this outcrop, cross another brook, then swing right and climb up the face of a large rock outcrop to Ritterbush Camp. The camp, a frame building with bunks for about eight people, was constructed in 1933 and is maintained by the Laraway Section of the Green Mountain Club.

To reach Devil's Gulch, follow the Long Trail south behind the camp. The trail swings left, then right, and enters the gulch through a narrow passage in the rocks. Devil's Gulch is an interesting geological feature, full of boulders and overgrown with ferns, many species of which can be found in the cool rock crevices and overhangs.

After enjoying this enchanting site, take the Long Trail north back to VT 118.

Note: Ritterbush Camp will be removed in fall 1998. A new shelter will be located just south of Devil's Gulch, off a short spur trail.

48

Belvidere Mountain via Forester's Loop

Total distance: 7.9-mile loop

Hiking time: 5 hours

Vertical rise: 2100 feet

Rating: Strenuous

Map: USGS 7.5' Hazen's Notch

Belvidere Mountain, famous for its asbestos mine, has a fire tower that provides excellent views of northern Vermont.

The acquisition of 1946 acres of land, including the summits of Belvidere Mountain, Haystack Mountain, and Tillotson Peak, was the Green Mountain Club's first major land purchase in its Long Trail Protection Campaign in northern Vermont. This valuable property, embracing 3 miles of the Long Trail, 4 miles of side trails, Tillotson Camp, and Lockwood Pond, is a significant purchase that has protected valuable natural and trail resources as well as helped the club move toward its overall goal of creating a protected corridor for the Long Trail.

How to Get There
Take VT 100 to Eden Mills, where you turn left in the center of town (0.0) and proceed uphill past the old Vermont Asbestos Group Mine entrance at 3.5 miles. At 5.0 miles take a sharp left onto a gravel road, where there is a sign for the "Frank Post Trailhead" just after the turn. At the last house, keep right onto the one-lane road to the old log landing at 5.6 miles, where you can park your car.

The Trail
Take the blue-blazed Frank Post Trail, which enters the woods and may be muddy at first. At 0.2 mile turn left onto an old road. Note the turn arrow as you will be returning via this trail. Follow the road uphill until you reach the junction of the Forester's Trail at 0.6 mile. This will be the trail you take on your return.

Turn right to remain on the Frank Post Trail. The old road begins to climb and is washed out in places. You reach a plateau at 1.4 miles, then follow easier grades until you climb a steep sidehill and pass through an area of birches. At 1.9 miles you cross a deep rock gully with moss-covered rock outcrops. Continue up a steep

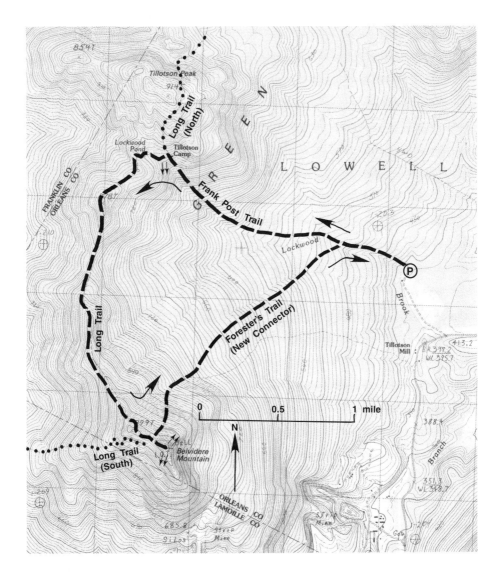

ascent out of this gully until you reach another deep gully with a brook. You will find these gullies beautiful, cool, and refreshing on a hot summer day. After ascending out of the second gully, you reach Tillotson Camp at 2.0 miles.

Tillotson Camp was built in 1939 by the Green Mountain Club. Enjoy a break at the shelter and a limited view to the east. Save lunch for the summit, which

the sign notes is 3 more miles.

Leaving the shelter, follow the white-blazed Long Trail south to the left of the shelter. This area is quite wet. Watch for moose tracks as you cross a water-flow outlet of the beaver pond. You soon reach Lockwood Pond. This high-elevation pond, called an alpine tarn, is the headwaters of the Missisquoi River, which flows north into Canada.

Lockwood Pond

Follow the Long Trail left of the pond until you begin a steep climb away from the pond at 2.5 miles. Look behind you for good views. Follow the ridgeline up, down, and across numerous plateaus. Be careful in this section because the trail is frequently wet and slippery. At 4.8 miles you reach the junction of the Forester's Trail. At this junction follow the blue-blazed summit spur trail 0.2 mile up to the Belvidere fire tower.

In 1919 a summit lookout station was established with the construction of a cabin, telephone lines, tower, and trail. In 1938 a hurricane blew down the old tower, and a new steel tower was built. In 1968 a new trailer-type cabin was airlifted by helicopter to the summit. The tower was operated until about 1970, when airplane patrols replaced many fire towers. The current tower was renovated into a public lookout tower by the Green Mountain Club in 1982.

From the tower there are excellent views: To the north, Tillotson Peak and Haystack Mountain are in the foreground, with the summit station on Jay Peak directly behind Haystack, and Little Jay to the left; to the east you can see the entire White Mountain range, from Mount Moosilauke in the south to the Presidentials in the north; to the southeast are Lake Eden, Green River Reservoir, and the Worcester Range from Mount Hunger to Elmore Mountain; to the southwest is the Green Mountain range, including Mount Abraham, Camel's Hump, Mount Mansfield, Madonna Mountain, Whiteface Mountain, Butternut Mountain, and finally, Laraway Mountain; to the west are the Cold Hollow Range and the Adirondack Mountains.

After enjoying the view, return to the junction of the Forester's Trail. From this junction, the Long Trail goes south 2.8 miles to VT 118. Instead, take the Forester's Trail, which was cut for the forest fire watchers who used the mountain tower. Descend along this steep trail—being careful because it is sometimes overgrown and wet. At 6.0 miles you reach an arrow on a tree that points left onto the newly relocated lower portion of the Forester's Trail. The trail follows a small brook, which you cross at 6.2 miles, and then heads away from the brook. The trail then enters a new-growth forest containing numerous logging road crossings. Be careful to stay on the main trail as you cross several of these roads and small brooks.

At 6.7 miles descend into a gully and follow a larger brook with nice cascades. Cross the brook, and continue until you reach the junction of the Frank Post Trail at 7.3 miles. Turn right and return to the parking area at 7.9 miles.

49

Jay Peak

Total distance: 3.5 miles

Hiking time: 4 hours

Vertical rise: 1680 feet

Rating: Moderate

Map: USGS 15' Jay Peak

Tram ascending Jay Peak

Jay Peak, the northernmost peak in the Green Mountain chain, was named in honor of John Jay, the first Chief Justice of the United States, who was instrumental in settling a controversy between the state of Vermont and the state of New York. Jay Peak, 3 miles of the Long Trail, and the Jay Peak Ski Area are all included in the 1390-acre Jay State Forest, which is managed primarily for recreation, wildlife, and watershed protection. An enclosed aerial tramway at the Jay Peak Ski Area allows year-round visits to the summit, so expect a few other visitors.

How to Get There

The trailhead parking area for 15 cars is at the height-of-land on the south side of VT 242, approximately 1.4 miles west of the Jay Peak Ski Area and 6.6 miles east of Montgomery Center.

The Trail

Follow the white-blazed Long Trail north up the bank opposite the parking lot. At the beginning of the trail you reach the Atlas Valley Shelter, a small lean-to not designed for overnight use. Made from plywood and plywood cores donated by the Atlas Valley Company, the shelter was pre-

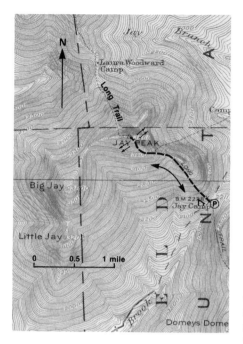

fabricated at the company's Morrisville plant and assembled on the site by members of the Green Mountain Club in 1967.

Continue your hike past the south end of a loop trail to Jay Camp, a frame cabin constructed in 1958 and maintained by the Green Mountain Club. Go straight at the junction, climb gradually, then more steeply, through a hardwood forest, and pass the north end of the Jay Camp spur trail. Continue your ascent on the main trail through a birch grove, along the hillside, and across a field of birches and ferns. Turn left at 1.0 mile to avoid the ski area, and hike over some steep ledges that parallel the ski trails. Turn left again at 1.2 miles, and continue a steep climb until you emerge on a ski trail. Hike directly across the ski trail, enter the rocks, and climb steeply, at times rock scrambling, to the summit at 1.7 miles.

On the summit is the upper station of the Jay Peak Tramway. Please respect the buildings and property. On a clear day there are views of Canada to the north, the Adirondack Mountains to the west, the White Mountains to the east, and most of northern Vermont. The large lake to the northeast is Lake Memphremagog.

Hike back down the same way.

50

Black Creek and Maquam Creek Trails/ Missisquoi National Wildlife Refuge

Total distance: 2.7 miles

Hiking time: 1–2 hours

Vertical rise: 25 feet

Rating: Easy

Map: USGS 7.5' East Alburg

These self-guided nature trails are in the 5651-acre Missisquoi National Wildlife Refuge, which occupies much of the Missisquoi River delta and consists of marsh, open water, and wooded swamp. *Missisquoi*, an Abenaki word, means an area of "much waterfowl" and "much grass." The refuge was established in 1942 to provide feeding, nesting, and resting areas for migrating waterfowl. During the peak of the fall migration there may be as many as 22,000 ducks present on the refuge at one time. The largest concentrations of waterfowl occur during April, September, and October. A variety of other

birds are also present during spring, summer, and fall, including great horned owls, barred owls, ospreys, and an occasional bald eagle.

Remember to bring binoculars, and walk slowly and quietly so you don't disturb the birds and wildlife. Time needed to hike this 1.5-mile loop will vary depending on how long you stop to observe your surroundings.

How to Get There
From Swanton (0.0), drive 2.4 miles west on VT 78 to the National Wildlife Refuge headquarters on the left side of the road. Parking is located behind the office.

The Trail
Before you begin your hike, locate the large information board with a map of the refuge at the back of the parking area. A box at the board includes a trail map for the "Black Creek and Maquam Creek Trails" as well as other information pamphlets. Some of the signposts that line the nature trail are in disrepair and may be missing. Note that the information pamphlet's 1.5-mile trail distance does not include walking in and out on the mowed roadway.

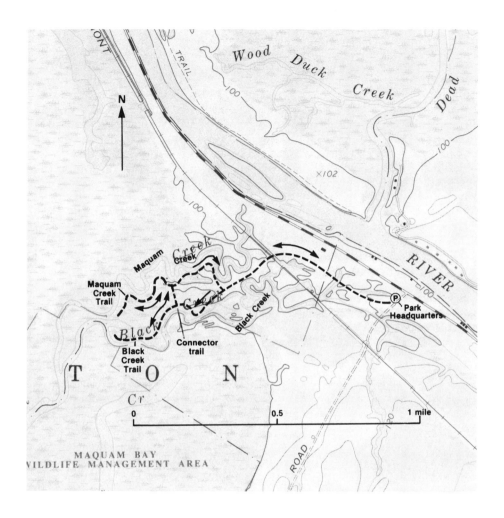

The trail starts at the information board and crosses the large meadow and railroad tracks into a wooded area. You immediately begin to hear birds as you follow the trail along the wide, mowed roadway and across the railroad tracks. Through the brush on your left, look for a very black meandering creek and possibly some beaver activity. Also, watch for game trails, which crisscross this section of the trail. On your right, you soon see the remnants of an old, now overgrown goose pen, constructed in the 1950s to establish a resident breeding flock of Canada geese.

At 0.3 mile another mowed roadway, the Maquam Creek Trail, enters from your right. You will return by this trail. Continue straight ahead to the end of the mowed roadway and the beginning of the Black Creek Trail, which follows the bank of the Black Creek. Black and slow moving, the creek lives up to its name. Take time to observe the reflections of the white birches, which make a nice contrast in the black water. Enjoy your time, but be prepared for a few (maybe many!) mosquitoes and blackflies during bug season. Look for the remnants of an old camp along the opposite bank.

At 0.6 mile you reach a trail junction, where a sign indicates a distance of 0.2 mile to the end of the Black Creek Trail. Follow along the Black Creek bank to the end of the trail. Turn around and return to the junction at 1.0 mile.

From the junction, take the connector trail to the Maquam Creek Trail at 1.1 miles. A sign indicates 0.5 mile to the end of this trail. Turn left and hike parallel to Maquam Creek. Look for lots of ducks along the creek as well as nesting boxes. The trail may be wet and/or flooded at times.

At 1.6 miles you reach Lookout Point, with a view of the creek and marsh. Return to the junction at 2.1 miles, and continue along the Maquam Creek Trail. The trail soon becomes more open and sunnier as you enter the mowed roadway. Just past a wet spot in the roadway look for the junction (at 2.4 miles) of the road on which you entered. Turn left, and hike back to Refuge Headquarters at 2.7 miles.

Index

Let Backcountry Guides Take You There

Our experienced backcountry authors will lead you to the finest trails, parks, and back roads in the following areas:

50 Hikes Series

50 Hikes in the Maine Mountains
50 Hikes in Southern and Coastal Maine
50 Hikes in Vermont
50 Hikes in the White Mountains
50 More Hikes in New Hampshire
50 Hikes in Connecticut
50 Hikes in Massachusetts
50 Hikes in the Hudson Valley
50 Hikes in the Adirondacks
50 Hikes in Central New York
50 Hikes in Western New York
50 Hikes in New Jersey
50 Hikes in Eastern Pennsylvania
50 Hikes in Central Pennsylvania
50 Hikes in Western Pennsylvania
50 Hikes in the Mountains of North Carolina
50 Hikes in Northern Virginia
50 Hikes in Ohio
50 Hikes in Michigan

Walks and Rambles Series

Walks and Rambles on Cape Cod and the
    Islands
Walks and Rambles in Rhode Island
More Walks and Rambles in Rhode Island
Walks and Rambles on the Delmarva Peninsula
Walks and Rambles in Southwestern Ohio
Walks and Rambles in Ohio's Western Reserve
Walks and Rambles in the Western Hudson
    Valley
Walks and Rambles on Long Island
Walks and Rambles in and around St. Louis

25 Bicycle Tours Series

25 Bicycle Tours in Maine
30 Bicycle Tours in New Hampshire
25 Bicycle Tours in Vermont
25 Mountain Bike Tours in Vermont
25 Bicycle Tours on Cape Cod and the Islands
25 Mountain Bike Tours in Massachusetts
30 Bicycle Tours in New Jersey
25 Bicycle Tours in the Adirondacks
25 Mountain Bike Tours in the Adirondacks
30 Bicycle Tours in the Finger Lakes Region
25 Bicycle Tours in the Hudson Valley
25 Bicycle Tours in the Twin Cities and
    Southeastern Minnesota
30 Bicycle Tours in Wisconsin
25 Mountain Bike Tours in the Hudson Valley
25 Bicycle Tours in Ohio's Western Reserve
25 Bicycle Tours in Maryland
25 Bicycle Tours on Delmarva
25 Bicycle Tours in and around Washington, D.C.
25 Bicycle Tours in Coastal Georgia and the
    Carolina Low Country
25 Bicycle Tours in the Texas Hill Country and
    West Texas

We offer many more books on hiking, fly-fishing, travel, nature, and other subjects. Our books are available at bookstores and outdoor stores everywhere. For more information or a free catalog, please call 1-800-245-4151 or write to us at The Countryman Press, PO Box 748, Woodstock, Vermont 05091. You can find us on the Web at www.countrymanpress.com.

An Invitation to Join the Green Mountain Club

Membership in the Green Mountain Club is open to all who enjoy the outdoors and have a special interest and pride in the mountains of Vermont. Since 1910, GMC volunteers, members, and staff have maintained the 445-mile Long Trail System, and they remain dedicated to managing and protecting the trails for future generations. Membership benefits include discounts on overnight fees at selected shelters, and on Club guidebooks and merchandise.

Two types of membership in the Green Mountain Club are available: at-large and section. Both at-large and section members are voting members of the GMC, support the Club with their dues, receive the quarterly *Long Trail News,* take part in clubwide activities and programs, volunteer on committees, and do trail maintenance.

At-large members support the mission of the Club but are not interested in joining a local group. They can still participate in trail maintenance and management through clubwide programs such as the Trail and Shelter Adopter program, serving on committees, or joining the Volunteer Long Trail Patrol.

GMCers who belong to one of the 13 sections are interested in meeting other members of the Club, enjoying outings year-round, or working with other section members on trail maintenance. They receive outing schedules and newsletters from the section they join.

Your GMC membership will support the maintenance of the Long Trail and its access trails, the protection of fragile natural areas, and the establishment of a permanent route for the Long Trail in northern Vermont.

Join the Green Mountain Club and contribute to the preservation of Vermont's Long Trail!

GMC Sections

Bennington, VT
Brattleboro, VT
Bread Loaf (Middlebury, VT)
Burlington, VT
Connecticut
Killington (Rutland, VT)
Laraway (Northern Vermont)
Manchester, VT
Montpelier, VT
New York, NY
Ottauquechee (Woodstock, VT)
Sterling (Morrisville/Stowe, VT)
Worcester, MA

Membership and Order Form

Name(s) _____

Address (street and mailing address, if different) _____

_____

Telephone number _____

Charge to _____ VISA _____ MC ($10 minimum, please)

Acct. no. _____

Signature _____

Please circle one membership category:

Individual* ....$27   Nonprofit or Youth Group..........$30

Family* ....$35   Business or Corporation........... $100

(includes children under 18)   *Volunteers/Limited Income may take a discount of $7*

Qty.	Title	Prices Member	Nonmember	Total
_____	*Long Trail Guide*	$11.95	$14.95	_____
_____	*Day Hiker's Guide to Vermont*	$7.95	$9.95	_____
_____	*Trail Map: Mt. Mansfield*	$3.15	$3.95	_____
_____	*Green Mountain Adventure* (softcover)	$7.95	$9.95	_____
_____	Long Trail Cloth Patch (for sleeve or pack)	$3.20	$4.00	_____
_____	GMC Patch	$1.80	$2.25	_____
_____	GMC Decal	$0.65	$0.75	_____
_____	*The Long Trail: A Footpath in the Wilderness*	Free	Free	_____
_____	*Winter Trail Use in the Green Mountains*	Free	Free	_____

Order Total _____

5% sales tax _____

(VT resident)

Postage _____

Subtotal _____

Membership Dues _____

Tax-Deductible Contribution _____

Total Amount Enclosed _____

Postage & Handling

Order of $5.00 and under.............. $1.50

Order of $5.01 to $20.00 .... $3.25

Order of $20.01 to $40.00 .... $3.75

Order of $40.01 and over $4.50

International orders.................add $2.00

(except Canada)

• Prices subject to change without notice.

• U.S. Funds only, please.

• If only free publications are ordered, please enclose a self-addressed, stamped ($0.55), legal size envelope.

Mail to: The Green Mountain Club, Inc., Route 100, RR 1 Box 650, Waterbury Center, VT 05677